"Theology that cannot be preached is not of much value. That one of our leading theologians can also present his message from a pulpit tells a great deal about the quality of his theology. This book will be welcomed by all who want a deeper note sounded in the pulpits of America."

—GERALD KENNEDY,
Bishop of the Methodist Church,
Los Angeles Area

the author

Nels F. S. Ferré is a widely known theologian, teacher, writer and preacher. Abbot Professor of Christian Theology at Andover Newton Theological School, Dr. Ferré is the author of SEARCHLIGHTS ON CONTEMPORARY THEOLOGY, STRENGTHENING THE SPIRITUAL LIFE, MAKING RELIGION REAL, and many other books.

GOD'S
NEW
AGE

A Book of Sermons

other books by *NELS F. S. FERRÉ*

GOD'S
NEW
AGE

A Book of Sermons

---

by NELS F. S. FERRÉ

ABBOT PROFESSOR OF CHRISTIAN THEOLOGY

ANDOVER NEWTON THEOLOGICAL SCHOOL

HARPER & BROTHERS PUBLISHERS, NEW YORK

GOD'S NEW AGE

to

BELLE CHAPMAN MORRILL
poet and partner in prayer

CONTENTS

PREFACE

Life is unpredictable. I never thought that I should publish a volume of sermons. Two things changed my mind. "Peter Parson" (W. B. J. Martin) both personally and in his column in the *British Weekly* challenged me to do so. I have selected two of the sermons I preached in his pulpit in Edinburgh: "The City of Confusion" and "Thanks Be to God."

When a few years ago *Newsweek* carried my name among ten preachers who have helped to change the religious situation in America to a strong resurgence of the Christian faith, I was thunderstruck, for, quite frankly, I have never thought of myself as even a good preacher. My main concern has been with writing and with teaching, and some lecturing. Preaching has been comparatively incidental and has never received the attention I have given the other three activities. Therefore I knew that the inclusion of my name was partly symbolic as a theologian who believes profoundly in preachable theology, but more because of the reality and the power of the message God has given me. Certainly it was not on account of any homiletical skill of mine. Rather, the strength of faith was revealed in weakness. Therefore I have come to feel more and more that not to publish is for me to be personally oversensitive and self-protective. Earthen vessels do carry the exceedingly precious Gospel that the glory might be of God.

Another matter also caused me to hesitate. I prefer to

preach from notes, not from a manuscript, preparing myself mostly on long walks, preaching and praying as I walk. The sermons prepared in this way are natural and communicate well, but when I see the result as taken on tape I realize how utterly informal they are. Nevertheless I have included a few of these for the record. Other sermons have been written in advance and gone over innumerable times before being preached. They are far smoother and perhaps "read" better, but something of my freedom and spontaneity is lost. I have been concerned that the sermon that has received the most favorable comment on publication is the very one that I have been wondering about including. The weight of the judgment of the editor of the periodical who had received the comments made me swallow my own opinion and include it in this work. I let the reader guess which sermon it is!

Several of these sermons have been preached at the Chicago Sunday Evening Club. What a challenge this pulpit is year after year! Others have been preached in universities and colleges such as Harvard, Cornell, Princeton, and Duke, as a "coming up" sermon at the University of London, in Mansfield Chapel, Oxford University in England, and in churches, some in Britain, but mostly in the United States and Canada. But I challenge any reader to pick where the sermons have been preached! I am convinced that theology can be preached and must be preached everywhere. "Peter Parson's" urging me to publish is in line with his conviction that we need more theological meat in our message. I was a bit disconcerted, however, when *The Pulpit* carried a lead article, "Can Eggheads Preach?" immediately followed by a sermon of mine!

A number of these sermons have been published, some under different titles, and I am grateful to the following periodicals for their further use:

The Upper Room Pulpit, "I Am Sure" and "The City of Confusion"; *The Pulpit,* "The Christian Victory ("Thanks Be To God"), "Thou Art the Christ" ("The True Christ"), and "God's New Age"; *The Christian Evangelist,* "Not of

Man, Nor By Man" ("Not of Men"); *The Peabody Reflector,* "The Christian Victory" ("Thanks Be To God"); *The Pulpit Digest,* "The God Who Makes All Things New" ("All Things New for the New Year"); *The United Church Herald,* "This Is the Time of Decision" ("Expanding Horizons").

As I grow older and our historical situation becomes ever more critical, I live increasingly for the coming of God's new age. The sermon bearing this title indicates my main desire, beyond mere human drives, for publishing these sermons. Indeed, inescapably I realize that Christmas is God's answer. I have no real hope for human beings or for history apart from the God who came as the fullness of time in the universal love of God in Christ Jesus our Lord.

GOD'S
NEW
AGE

A Book of Sermons

CHAPTER 1

God's New Age

Peter continued knocking. . . . ACTS 12:16

Peter had been put in prison by Herod and therefore the early church was gathered in a room to pray for Peter. Surely these disciples prayed for his safe release, within the will of God, and for his speedy deliverance that he might again be their leader and spokesman. God did deliver him. God did answer their prayers! Now Peter stood outside the door knocking to be let in. The answer to their prayer stood outside the door begging entrance.

Down ran Rhoda, the maid, to answer the door. But when she heard Peter's voice, for joy she ran away to tell the rest. Our dear sentimental Rhodas, who for joy keep the Peters standing outside! There are many sentimentalists in religion who for the joy of it do nothing about it. Instead they keep the answer to prayer standing outside the door knocking.

But when Rhoda came to the praying disciples, they were no better, either. They brushed her aside, calling her mad and saying it *couldn't* be so. Why, after all they were just praying for his release! But when she insisted that it was so, they said that it must be Peter's ghost. That is all most people expect from God in answer to their prayers. They get a ghost of what they pray for; not the real thing.

But when the disciples finally opened up, there was Peter and they were amazed! The answer was at the door even while they prayed.

Even so, we keep God's answer at the door by not believing him. I am persuaded that all things are in God's hands, that he alone is the ruler of the nations and of human lives, but that we seldom have our eyes opened to his reality and power. Therefore even when we confess and pray, we don't really believe. We keep God's answer standing knocking, knocking at the door.

The prophets in Israel interpreted history in the light of God. They did not first talk of the armies of Cyrus or the battles of Nebuchadnezzar, but they spoke of the arm of the Lord God. They saw history in the light of man's obedience or disobedience to God. God acted. That is how they viewed history. In the same way the Reformers spoke of the mighty acts of God. For them not church nor state, but God and God alone reigned supreme in history. All that happened they understood in the light of God.

We have need to return to the power of the Reformation. It needs the strength of the prophets of the Bible. Let's begin to see what is happening as in God's sight.

Our earthly lives have a ceiling and a floor. We cannot get rid of our problems of history by flying into heaven. We'll bump our heads on the ceiling of history that God put there to make us face our problems. That's what earth is for.

But history has a floor, too. If we go through that floor we perish. Individuals commit suicide and nations are destroyed.

But between the ceiling and the floor we can make a world either good to live in or heavy with hell. A life can be high or low. A family can be a community of high, happy lives or of low lives of sin and horror. A church can be a fellowship that heals and attracts, or a place of strife and tension. Our nation can be strong or weak, depending on our way of living. What determines the kind of life, family, church, or nation is finally our vision of God and how we respond to him.

Therefore, without either optimism or despair, let us look at history in the light of God, as did the prophets of the Bible and the Reformers in their day.

When I first moved into my beloved Southland, while

traveling on a train I saw behind a dark curtain in the dining car a gentle, strong, serene face above a clerical collar. I wanted to join my fellow preacher, but was afraid of embarrassing him. All the same, I suffered and suffered for the conditions that kept us apart. Suffering, I returned and told my friends that I was going to pray and work to have God remove that curtain of separation. My friends said, "Be realistic, that curtain will never come down!" Within a few months God took it away to stay. I thanked God for his mighty deed. That is how the Hebrew prophets, that is how the Reformers looked at human affairs. God did it.

Of course, the Supreme Court helped, but *God* did it. That is the prophetic understanding. How much we need it today. Since then what seemed impossible has happened. Jim Crow laws generally and even segregation in schools have become unlawful. God has broken through heavy barriers. Of course there is lack of human acceptance. Of course there is trouble. Of course there are problems beyond belief. Are we not human and sinful? But neither state troops nor dynamiters can keep back the arm of God when he lifts it to help. *God* did it, and he will keep doing the incredible, not only through law, but even more through love, as soon as we get ready to answer the knocking at the door.

The answer to better race relations is knocking now. Many have prayed and worked for a better age in this respect. Too easily we can descend into deep trouble if we reject God— which is a strong possibility—but by God's grace we can win, bit by bit, or leap by leap.

Or take the case of the Iron Curtain. For years my children used to pray, "God, remove the Iron Curtain." Once I happened to express the hope that someday I might preach in Russia. The so-called realists raged back at me, "Russia is totalitarian. Never will they let a Christian preacher in; be realistic! Come to your senses!" "God can do it; can't he?" was my reply, and since then, although I myself have not been, many of our best preachers from the United States and from Europe have visited and preached there! Let these events be symbols for us, conveying the reality and power of God.

And despite cold war tensions, there are still signs of hope for new understanding. Performing artists, organized groups, and ordinary tourists move more freely between East and West; scientific meetings include delegates from both sides; issues such as the recognition of Communist China are debated with more reason and less heat. *God* can lift the Iron and Bamboo Curtains; God has done so much already; God will do far more, if we trust him and repent before him.

Many of us have been praying that the underdeveloped countries of the world be helped. We care for them, for we are Christians. Even on a lower level, how can we have peace when 50 per cent of the world's population has 9 per cent of its income? And now the two greatest nations on earth are competing in a so-called "cold war" to help these countries economically. What an irony of history? No, what a miracle of God's grace! Over a third of the world's population has found a new freedom *within our generation*. History is on the move, yes, for *God* is *on the march*. It used to be believed that the mightiest guns won the final battles. Now when world war is becoming no option we know a new power of world opinion.

We had better be awake, or we won't *be!* I am sure that God has shifted the very gears of human existence, offering us bloom or blight. We must now rise to a new spiritual and social maturity as peoples of the world or perish. We must break the power of war before we are ourselves broken in pieces. But we can do it only through faith. God alone is now our refuge and strength, the guide and power of the new age that can be ours. Here is what D. F. Fleming, distinguished author and long-time head of the department of political science at Vanderbilt University, has written (*British Weekly*, May 2, 1957) :

"Some time in the next few decades the human race is due to extinguish itself in one last fratricidal conflict. This statement is not made to shock readers. It is set down to record the end toward which all history points, the *finale* toward which we have been moving with constantly accelerating speed since 1914. This pitiful finish to man's long ascent from barbarism is not indicated because he is still a savage at heart. Indeed, there are countless millions of decent, peaceable people living, all the way around the world, people of many faiths and ideologies, who are good neighbors to each other as individuals. The trouble arises out of the fact that these same neighborly people are organized in national states, and the primary function of the state is defense against other states or aggression against them, depending upon circumstances."

War is not Christian; we all know that. War is no answer to our problems today; we all know that. But we seem caught up in a juggernaut we cannot control. We are like the four-year-old child we read about recently who stepped into a multi-ton bulldozer and knew how to start it but not how to stop it. Starting it gave him a sense of achievement and power, but when it was out of control he was terrified. On he went, crushing cars and finally landing in the cellar of a house that had been there until he came!

We will land in the cellar of a civilization that used to be there unless we can conquer war. Here is a creative task. But it is too big for us. We are like the four-year-old with a bulldozer, hurtling away out of control. We see death ahead and are terrified. Stop we must and cannot. But God can stop war if we *let* him, by trusting, obeying, and working. God can crush the grip of the military on the people of Russia and America and China before it is too late.

Once I labored to open a coconut, and how it frustrated me! Then in the zoo in Miami I saw one tossed to an elephant. He barely leaned his foot on it and crack!

God's power is like that. He waits only for the five in Sodom for whom he will spare the city. We need people to stand up for God's right over our freedom to control our states. We need international and supernational control.

In the atomic age sovereign nations are more out of date

than sovereign States of the Union. The United Nations are at least a feeble beginning of the United World, the co-operative community of mankind. A herculean task, yes; impossible and visionary, yes; but our only way now. As James P. Warburg, voluminous writer on foreign policy, has kept saying to us, it is too soon for world government; but it is too late for anything else.

Shall we perish or shall we have peace? Your faith in God, your prayers, your vote make a difference. I, for one, choose to believe against all reason based on past history that God can, and will if we let him, break the bow and the hydrogen bomb, too, and make of what could be sheer destruction a better day for our children's children. Cobalt bombs for death; or atomic energy for a whole new industrial order, delivering man from drudgery and challenging him to a new, creative way of living, with property and automation, and not man, the slave of the world's needs. Which shall it be? I choose God and God's new age.

God has shifted the gears of history. Either we learn to drive at a new rate, his rate of co-operative community, or we learn to die by dying. God longs to save us, awaiting only our willingness to be helped and to help within the freedom and faithfulness in community under God for which we are made and for which we must work.

But what of religion itself? God's new age can come there, too. Science rightly interpreted need no longer undermine authentic faith. Many top leaders in science and advanced leaders in religion are coming together in a common openness. The religions of the world are making feeble beginnings, they too, to sit down in a common living room to face one another.

As they learn to know one another, they can come to understand one another; and when they do—God grants a speedy acquaintance! They will discover that the love of God that came in Christ is man's basic need and alone can save him, in this world and in the world to come. True Christian faith has nothing to fear, for love throws out fear

and, as A. H. Maslow says in *Motivation and Personality,*
love is as much of a human necessity as salt.

What, however, of the branches of the Christian faith?
Are they not bitterly apart?

Fundamentalists, Liberals, and Neo-orthodox all are beginning to seek together. In a leading Fundamentalist magazine
(*Christian Life,* March, 1956), in an article "Where Is Conservative Theology Going?" outstanding young Fundamentalist scholars from all over the country declared that they
no longer want to be known as Fundamentalists, but as
Evangelicals, that they can no longer subscribe to a narrow
view of inspiration and that they will accept everything that
legitimate science offers. Their authority is going to be
"God's redemptive love, wisdom and power as revealed in
Jesus Christ." Well, that's mine and has been for years, and
was the original center of the Christian faith, and always will
remain so!

When the Liberals were described in the next issue of the
same magazine, they were seen as changing even more rapidly
from making experience and human reason ultimate to
biblical faith and to God's love in Christ. I think this is true.
Liberalism is undergoing a profound transformation back toward the center of the Reformation and the Christian faith.

Even the Neo-orthodox are asking where they shall go
after they have knocked down all kinds of idols. Neo-
orthodoxy—some call it a sophisticated Fundamentalism and
some call it more biblically centered Liberalism—is also seeking a steady and powerful center. There is only one center;
God in Christ as universal Holy Love; or put the center
differently: *God is faithful!*

God is moving not only upon the face of the waters, but
in the hearts of men. I believe that we can come to a more
mature and creative era of co-operative seeing, at least in
Protestantism. God speed that day! Will you help prepare
in your life for his new age?

But what of Catholicism! Trust God for that hurdle, too.
When God puts the bulldozer of his loving might under any

movement, something cracks. He who is cracking our heads together as Protestants and as world religions will surely not spare the great old Catholic Church. Thank God for the faith in God and in life after death the Catholic neighbors have, and become one with them in love and faith for God's new age.

Let God do the rest. He who raised up Moses and Luther will raise up his Savonarolas and St. Francises to work his co-operative work. Who knows what a modern-day pope can do to open Christian-wide opportunities for ecumenicity? The little blade of grass cracks the sidewalk. The little act of love cracks the hardest institution. As Luther said, "Light God's little lantern!" Trust God for the sun.

This, then, is our faith. God's new age can come and *will*, if you let it. It cannot and will not come *easily*. We shall never drift into it. But it will come when God the eternal Victor is *let* use your freedom and mine. Our security is in the faithfulness of God. Our freedom is in his love. He will keep us safe only as we move forward at his fast clip.

When I was a boy in Sweden I used to ride a bicycle. How hard I pumped to get a little bit farther up each time on the steep hills of my childhood! Then in the summer of 1956 I took my family to Europe especially for my children to see Sweden. We drove a big American car, a rented Chevrolet! Before I knew it I was over the hills.

We talk of overcoming tensions, climbing the steep hills of difficulty. Without muscular tensions we could not move; we could not lift an arm. The problem is not tensions, but destructive misdirected tensions. What we need is *relaxed tension.*

How much tension, and how relaxed, when the motor of the car purred complacently over the hills! Let God be *your* motor. Learn to use relaxed tension. We often hear "God go with you!" *He* is all willing. I say to you, *go with God* into his new age!

God's new age is waiting for you. God's answer to your prayers is knocking at the door. Let Peter in!

CHAPTER 2
Thanks Be to God

Thanks be to God, which giveth us the victory through our Lord Jesus Christ. I CORINTHIANS 15:57

My text is a cry of victory—Christian victory. Any sermon preached on this text should be sung. This sermon is no philosophy, no exposition, no exhortation. It is a cry of victory, a celebration of the reality and presence of God in human history and beyond human history.

Christ is the Lord of Love. In Jesus, God himself has drawn near to save the world. By giving us eternal life he has conquered death. This same eternal Christ, if we let him, will enter our lives to make us victors over all the enemies of life and to destroy for us death itself. Therefore let us sing God's victory in Christ:

Thanks be to God, which giveth us the victory through our Lord Jesus Christ.

Thanks be to God, which giveth us the victory through our Lord Jesus Christ, that the faithfulness of his love is more dependable than the faithlessness of our fears!

To live in fear is to live in the shadow of death, for God is love and love is life. Our fears, too, are either grounded or not grounded. Freud knew that while it was natural to see snakes in the grass it was unnatural to see them in bed. Most suffering from fear comes in a form of anxiety below real reason for fear. As a matter of fact, the worst worriers are those who seek one object of fear after another in order to "objectify" anxiety. They suffer far more from snakes in bed than from snakes in the grass.

Such fear resulting from insecurity is conquered by God-security; perfect love casts out fear.

In all days but particularly in ours there is, however, real reason for fear. We all know how precarious life is. We feel the threat both of personal calamity and of political or military catastrophe. Yet even here we can trust God. Those who know the meaning and the power of the Cross can accept whatever comes to them by a surrendered reliance on the faithfulness of God, for God has conquered and will conquer the worst by the best. If God is for us, who can be against us?

My saintly mother, when once I was privileged to visit her, came to meet me at the door and before I had put my bags down, she queried, "Nels, is God all good; can I say anything too good about him?" My reply was instant. "No mother, you can't; God is all for us and for us all always!" "Thank you, dear," she replied, "what more can I need?"

Thanks be to God, which giveth us the victory through our Lord Jesus Christ, that the faithfulness of his love is more dependable than the faithlessness of our fears!

Thanks be to God, which giveth us the victory through our Lord Jesus Christ, that the length of his love outlasts the stubbornness of our sin!

All of us have sinned and come short of the glory of God. We are never fully awake to reality until we wake up to self and determine to fight it. The more we know both the reality of Christ and of ourselves the more we are overwhelmed by the depth and stubbornness of sin. Then we long to be rid of our load, to be free from the burden of sin.

My father sat by his Swedish organ day after day and sang a song which translated would read "One day without sin I shall awake!" At my father's funeral my brother braved that song for a solo, as expressing the deepest longing of father's life. Our father knew the Savior from sin and therefore he could shout:

Thanks be to God, which giveth us the victory through

our Lord Jesus Christ, that the length of his love outlasts the stubbornness of our sin!

Thanks be to God, which giveth us the victory through our Lord Jesus Christ, that the strength of his purpose is more durable than the straying of our aimlessness!

Whenever I think of the fact I am astonished how little time and energy, let alone wisdom, we give deliberately to pursue the path of God. Even our efforts to promote the common good are exceedingly scattered. How much time do we spend as communities to discover and do the will of God? No! The planner and executor of most our lives and of history as a whole is not we, but God. His great plan holds our lives together and directs the nations more deeply than conscious intention.

As a young boy I heard a great preacher from London so old he had to sit in the pulpit, but his message I can never forget: "Write on my tombstone these words only: 'He taught men to reckon on God.' " However much we may stray, underneath our lives and history are the everlasting arms. Therefore let us make melody with our hearts:

Thanks be to God, which giveth us the victory through our Lord Jesus Christ, that the strength of his purpose is more durable than the straying of our aimlessness!

Thanks be to God, which giveth us the victory through our Lord Jesus Christ, that the rest in his peace is more real than the restlessness of our conflicts!

How many of us are weary of wearing tensions at work, among friends when we are supposed to have fun, perhaps even at home. How many are tired to death of war and the threat of war? How many are anxious over the outcome in the South of the Supreme Court's decision ordering desegregation? How many are dismayed by denominational rivalry in days such as these?

Without conflict and tensions there can be no growth either in persons or in community. Christ does not deliver

us from conflict but makes us victorious in conflict by giving us his own self. Whatever is born of God overcomes
the world. This is the Christian victory, even our faith.
Through this faith and the Holy Presence we come to know
the peace which surpasses knowledge and which guards
our hearts and minds in Christ Jesus. Through the power
given to us we come to know the peace which the world
can neither give nor take away. It is the whirlwind's heart
of peace, not seen from the outside but known from the
inside.

Even the threat of war cannot dismay us within the peace
deeper than death; and shall not the God who raised up
judges rightly to interpret the law of the land and of God
also raise up strong and wise men to implement the
decision of the Supreme Court? Nothing can disturb a
peace purchased on the Cross and as sure as the heart of
God. Therefore with quiet calm we whisper:

*Thanks be to God, which giveth us the victory through
our Lord Jesus Christ, that the rest in his peace is more real
than the restlessness of our conflicts!*

*Thanks be to God, which giveth us the victory through
our Lord Jesus Christ, that the height of his hope erases the
depths of our hopelessness!*

We live in an age largely bereft of hope. Gone is the
old optimism. Come is the new despair. We have been told
that never before were the commencement speakers at
our colleges and universities more grave, even despairing,
than at this time. "Realism" reigns. A student from the
London School of Economics told me at a seminar in Wind-
sor, England, that we should thank God for our age of
disillusionment. Having no hope, he said, we have nowhere
to fall!

Contrast such feelings with those of another dark age
when our faith was young: Always abounding hope; a
sure hope; "the God of hope fill you with all peace and joy
in believing, that ye may abound in hope, through the

power of the Holy Ghost," (Rom. 15:13). Without hope
in God we have a right to despair, but standing on the
promises of God, even when our hearts are weighted down,
we repeat to ourselves: "Hope thou in God for I shall praise
him who is the health of my countenance and my God"
(Ps. 42:11). Therefore with hope born anew we sing:

*Thanks be to God, which giveth us the victory through
our Lord Jesus Christ, that the height of his hope erases the
depths of our hopelessness!*

*Thanks be to God, which giveth us the victory through
our Lord Jesus Christ, that the surety of his promises is
safer than the struggle of our doubts!*

Doubt is good when it serves growth; doubt is bad when
it results from sin. Most of our doubt has been due to
spiritual rather than to intellectual causes. Intellectual doubt
we must honor. The doubt which is a smokescreen, to
shut God out of our lives, we must destroy. Our age is at
least beginning to doubt its own doubts. It sees its own false
certainties for what they are. Our idols stand impotent:
our faith in knowledge apart from commitment; our faith
in science apart from repentance; our faith in man apart
from God. Recently an outstanding social scientist from
whom I should never have expected such words exploded
that he wanted men of faith to say what they believed without quibbling and qualifying. This is an age when we need
to decide about ultimates and to live them.

Some of us have come to find in the Christian faith—
God's ever-faithful love, symbolized and summarized by
the Cross and the Resurrection—a light that never was on
land or sea. Our sins were forgiven when we accepted this
light and in it we overcame our intellectual doubts. Therefore we affirm the Christian victory of light!

*Thanks be to God, which giveth us the victory through
our Lord Jesus Christ, that the surety of his promises is
safer than the struggle of our doubts!*

Thanks be to God, which giveth us the victory through our Lord Jesus Christ, that the freedom of his service is more liberating than the fancy of our willfulness!

Aldous Huxley has described how the cry for freedom among his own youthful associates was in reality a clamor for irresponsibility. Why fence in our drives? Why not enjoy life to the full? He knows better now, he confesses! Edgar Sheffield Brightman had a candidate for the doctorate writing on the nature of ultimate reality. The student finally told Dr. Brightman that intellectually he had come to the conclusion that God was the most adequate answer to the riddle of reality but that he would not accept this answer because, if he should decide that there was a God, he could no longer do as he pleased. How many are there who come to the same conclusion, although below conscious awareness and honest acknowledgment?

Those who have found the Christian victory, however, know that in acceptance of God's will is freedom. Passivity gives power. To be free is to effect God's purpose for us and to express our whole nature. Freedom comes with fulfillment of self and society within the will of God for all men. True liberty is the one with which Christ has set us free. Seeking freedom for self we become slaves; becoming slaves of Christ we find ourselves startlingly free, and freely we exult:

Thanks be to God, which giveth us the victory through our Lord Jesus Christ, that the freedom of his service is more liberating than the fancy of our willfulness!

Thanks be to God, which giveth us the victory through our Lord Jesus Christ, that the certainty of his health is more healing than the coddling of our sorrow!

A friend writing from Oklahoma related that his physician believed cancer to be a kind of theological disease, as mysterious as the control of life itself, growth run riot. A physician friend of mine also challenged me, *as a theologian,* to solve the problem of cancer. I have, however, no idea on the subject. Certainly some of the most saintly and at least seemingly most controlled people die of cancer. One thing is certain, however, and that is that there is a spiritual dimension to illness. A physician who had worked long on the subject of so-called psychosomatic medicine confided to me his conviction that there is a third even more important aspect to his problem—the spiritual.

Another physician reported that he had found the great majority of his patients suffering from no physical cause at all! Those who suffer from a physical cause, moreover, can alter their condition considerably by means of their will to live, their deepest purpose for living. Some of us have been healed by physicians. God uses them continually for his healing ministry. We have also found deep healing in faith. The early church practiced healing. On no subject, I believe, must we be more careful, but of this I am sure, that the church of Jesus Christ needs again to know the power of a healing ministry by every means at its command: medical, mental, and spiritual. The coddling of our sorrows increases our illness; the immortal medicine of God's love heals them.

Even when there is no help from illness, either from doctor or from believing prayer, there is available a new heart of faith to bear up under illness and to know the Healer beyond every harm. Victorious faith should again know the strain of victory:

Thanks be to God, which giveth us the victory through our Lord Jesus Christ, that the certainty of his health is more healing than the coddling of our sorrow!

Thanks be to God, which giveth us the victory through our Lord Jesus Christ, that the Light of Life everlasting refutes the lie of our death!

We know that we all die. The Christian faith takes death, as an event, with complete seriousness. We are not by nature immortal. By nature we are all bound for death.

Nevertheless, when we know the Christian God, we know

that he calls us back to life again. We know that for those who believe in Jesus' Resurrection there is also resurrection for all. Death is birth! The New Testament speaks of "the birthpangs of death," of "the first-born from the dead." God lets us all be born to newness of life in order to face his inexorable judgment and his illimitable grace. In his hands we are safe, for there is no condemnation for those who are in Christ Jesus; nothing shall ever separate us from the love of God in Christ Jesus our Lord; God is not the God of the dead but of the living, for all live unto him.

What more can we ask? What more can we believe? Details of death and newness of life we cannot know now. They belong to a new existence, but we can know the God who is on both sides of the Great Divide. We can trust him. "The strife is o'er, the battle done; the victory of life is won."

My deepest experiences and my truest seeing require a far larger view of God than ever before. Our time and life here on earth are only a stammering beginning of God's great plan and purpose for us.

When we buried our daughter God was with us. Instead of gloom at the grave there was a Presence and a Power. Instead of an empty feeling there was the endless togetherness in Reality. What is here merely begun shall be continued in God's unemptiable time.

When we see the great Light of Life we cannot contain our singing; we must burst forth in triumph, caroling the Christian victory over all the enemies of life and over death itself:

Thanks be to God, which giveth us the victory through our Lord Jesus Christ, that the Light of Life everlasting refutes the lie of our death. Thanks be to God!

CHAPTER 3

The Golden Bowls

. . . golden bowls full of incense, which are the prayers of the saints. . . . REVELATION 5:8

What could be more dramatic than this little-known story in the Bible? We were reading it one morning for our family devotions when its truth burst upon me.

The prayers of the saints have evidently already been poured from the golden bowls upon the altar of God. Thereupon an angel mingles with these prayers the incense from his golden censer. "And the smoke of the incense rose with the prayers of the saints from the hand of the angel before God" (Rev. 8:4). This smoke rises well-pleasing to God; then the angel swiftly scoops up some of the fire from the altar and hurls it down on the earth; "and there were peals of thunder, loud noises, flashes of lightning, and an earthquake" (Rev. 8:5).

When saints pray, something real and important always happens. Genuine Christian prayer is not as though a woman should take cold water and throw it in a hot frying pan; it is much more as though a man should take a burning match and cast it into a gasoline tank. The power of true prayer is explosive.

Men of true prayer have been men of power for good. Jesus himself was a man of profound prayer. He prayed being baptized; he prayed healing; he prayed from early morning or all through the night as he ministered to people; he prayed on the Mount of Transfiguration; he prayed in Gethsemane; and he prayed dying.

Peter Taylor Forsyth, the British theologian, even attributes the atoning deity of Jesus to prayer. Surely if Jesus' freedom and victory over sin were both real, the interrelation of the divine and the human in Jesus could be kept together only by prayer. Professor Thomas Torrance of the University of Edinburgh once told me how an American graduate student, who had come there an exceedingly conservative Southerner, one day rushed up to him and exclaimed,

"Professor Torrance, I see Jesus' manhood now for the first time in my life. I can really believe that Jesus prayed."

Before this he had never been able to accept, deep down in his life, the New Testament account that Jesus prayed. Jesus, he had believed, was God, and God cannot pray! Now he understood the fuller meaning of the Word made flesh.

Paul prayed without ceasing. Read his letters and see how often and how importantly Paul mentions his praying. And how he begged others to pray for him!

You remember the account of the follower of St. Francis who pretended to be asleep and who, after all was quiet, observed the saint creep out of bed and pray all night, totally absorbed in his God and his all.

Loyola founded the Jesuit Order in and on prayer, and, if we go outside the Christian fold, Socrates, with whom the great age of Western thought began, could do nothing without consulting his "daemon," that is to say, without praying. Gandhi died on his way to prayer.

Dr. Nathaniel Micklem, former principal of Mansfield College, Oxford, has observed that whereas Descartes said, "I think, therefore I am," and the modern existentialists say, "I decide, therefore I am," the Christian knows the truth of the affirmation, "I pray, therefore I am." Man is right and real only in relation to God. Rabbi Samuel H. Dresner has said accordingly that "a man is as he prays."

Increasingly I learn that prayer is my most important occupation. Prayer is the work I do that lasts the longest and produces the most good results. I believe that if we pray true prayers, our prayers will be placed in the golden bowls before the altar of God, that God will be pleased by them, and that they will be returned to earth with inestimable power for good. The way to get our prayers placed in the golden bowls at the altar of God is to pray true Christian prayer. Our best model of Christian prayer is the one we know as the Lord's Prayer.

I

True prayer is first of all acknowledgment. "Our Father who art in heaven, hallowed be thy name." How hard it is for modern man truly to say that!

How hard it is for any one of us to find things real outside ourselves! Even people we know the best are mysteries to us. After nearly three decades of happy, intimate married life, my wife will say to me,

"Nels, I know you feel very strongly about (this or that) but for the life of me I can't understand why. I can't see any reason for it."

For my part, I know full well that on certain subjects she is going to react with deep feelings, and yet after all these years of living with her I can't figure out why. Why should she feel so strongly about things that make practically no difference to me?

If people who know each other long and closely can't really enter into the other person's life, how much more difficult it is for modern man to feel things real outside himself! How hard it is for those stuck in the rut of their own self-interest to recognize anything as really real and important beyond their own personal ambition or interest! How intensely difficult to acknowledge God to be real!

Modern man's doubts, I believe, are caused far more by his inability to acknowledge God than by a lack of intellectual grasp. Modern men—that is to say you and I—find it easiest to begin with the self as real, and hardest to acknowledge God as more real than ourselves. Descartes started with self-knowledge, with what Archbishop Temple called the Cartesian *faux pas*. Whitehead called the same tendency on the part of modern man the "subjectivistic bias."

Stéphane Mallarmé, a nineteenth-century French poet, said something to the following effect: In classical times God was real; he created the heavens and the earth, hanging each star and calling it by name; in the medieval world the stars were still there but they could be known only as man named them; in the modern world there are no stars except as man names them. Is that why prayer comes hard?

Once while living in Sweden I became closely acquainted with a brilliant young prize-winning author, who confessed that when he had finished a long writing project he always felt frustrated because he had no ultimate source to thank.

"I go out on my veranda," he mourned, "I lift up my manuscript, wanting to thank God, but he is never there to thank."

That is exactly modern man's problem. He is without God because he cannot acknowledge his reality.

An anecdote of uncertain origin fits my point precisely:

Three baseball umpires were arguing.

"I call balls and strikes exactly the way they come," said the first. He was an objectivist.

"I can't do that," replied the second. "I call them balls and strikes just the way I see them." He was a subjectivist.

But the third had an idea all his own.

"They are neither balls nor strikes," he declared, "until I call them." He was an existentialist.

That exactly is modern man's problem. Nothing is real or right for him unless he says so. He must call life's pitches. He is man-centered at the depths of his consciousness; yes, far into the formations of his unconscious, he has forgotten how to acknowledge that God is our Father. He cannot say, "Hallowed be thy name." No wonder that he cannot pray. Man's first requirement is to be brought to his knees in terms of his desperate need to acknowledge reality. May the acute crisis of mankind help us again to acknowledge God and to begin rightly to pray.

II

Prayer is also acceptance. "Thy kingdom come. Thy will be done on earth as it is in heaven." We need not only to acknowledge God by hallowing his name but also to accept his will.

What can be harder for modern man? We are democratic. To accept God's will, to *obey* him, goes contrary to the very grain of our being. After all, we *are* democratic. We don't believe in lords. We don't want the will of another imposed on us.

Bernard of Clairvaux in writing to the pope affirmed that love has no lord! If God is really Love, if he is our Father, how can we really own him to be Lord? Erich Fromm similarly has hammered home to us the truth that modern man cannot abide the authoritarian character structure.

What is our answer? If this world is to be the best medium for an indefinite number of people to grow together in freedom, there must be one will for all that provides the condition for such growth in freedom and for such exercise of freedom. God's will is no foreign imposition on our wills. His will is our own deepest and best will when we understand and come to ourselves.

One of my former colleagues, Everett Tilson, used to say that God requires obedience because he desires fellowship. It is just the way parents have to be morally strict with their children if they are going to grow up in happy freedom. License never leads to liberty.

The Gluecks of Harvard in their writings on juvenile delinquency have stated that the most effective guard against delinquency is a father who is at the same time both strict and loving. There are plenty of fathers who are "loving," and spoil their children into selfishness and crime. There are other fathers who are strict enough, whose children revolt against them and keep right on revolting against society into a life of crime. God is the Father who is both perfectly strict and perfectly loving. That is the reason that we can say, "Thy will be done on earth as it is in heaven."

But acceptance of the will of God must be a total acceptance. Partial loyalty to God is ultimate loyalty to some idol, really to some other god. Most of us do sin most of the time against the First Commandment, "Thou shalt have no other gods."

There are many who will follow the Lord halfway, claims Bernard of Clairvaux. They will give up wealth, friendship, and position, but it touches them too closely to disown their own selves. We can all join him in this affirmation. Augustine never found peace with God while he willed to will God's will—but not entirely and not yet!

The difficulty with the acceptance of God's will in prayer and then in life is that to accept him we must accept all others as well. God's will is for all and entirely. To accept God is to accept all our fellow men, generally and in particular. Walt Whitman urged that we refuse no one, like the sun that shines on all indiscriminately.

Karl W. Deutsch, a political scientist at Yale University, spent years investigating why some cultures were creative while others were not. He found one difference: a creative culture levels barriers; a deteriorating culture builds them. Thus in ancient Greek culture during the creative fifth century B.C. democracy was coming, and fast. When Greek civilization began to decay, however, we find Aristotle the last person to converse with a fisherman, and, at that, he spoke to him as a philosopher speaks to an object of research rather than as person to person.

I shall never forget an experience I had in Nashville, Tennessee. One Monday night at Scarritt College I addressed a group of Methodist "A-3's," composed largely of recent college graduates who had signed up as missionary recruits for three years of service in Africa. Among them that summer night happened to be a handsome young man, a visitor from the Union of South Africa, a Negro.

"How do you define the Christian faith?" he asked me in the question period.

I began to tick off on my fingers: God, Christ, the forgiveness of sin, and the fully inclusive and open society which is the nature of the true Christian church. I was unaware that the preceding day he had gone to church with the other A-3's and had been turned away at the door. In those days no Negro could be admitted into this "Christian" church.

He was too much of a gentleman to tell me this. When one of the group mentioned it to me later, I suffered and suffered. In my spirit I stood outside that church, shut out with him, suffering until I could stand it no longer and took both him and the people of that church into my arms of love and prayer to hold until we shall all become mature enough to accept all God's children. Until we do so we are not accepting God either.

There is no true Christian prayer until we are ready fully to accept God and one another. The right prescription for prayer includes "Thy kingdom come. Thy will be done in earth as it is in heaven." If our prayers are really to be placed in the golden bowls of the prayers of the saints, to be consecrated on the altar of God and returned with power to help the earth, we must pray true prayers. We must learn fully and wholeheartedly to accept God's will for all.

III

Prayer is also asking. "Give us this day our daily bread, and forgive us our debts as we forgive our debtors." True Christian prayer includes petition, asking for ourselves; and intercession, asking for others.

Some people are so sophisticated that they think we should never ask God for anything. God knows what we need, they claim, and our asking him is just a waste of time. Over and over again I hear sermons and discussions against petitionary prayer. I am glad that Jesus included it in his model prayer. He also affirmed, "How much more shall your Father

which is in heaven give good things to them that ask him"
(Matt. 7:11). Another account, to be sure, promises the
Holy Spirit instead of good things, but the likelihood is
that in the writing of the New Testament spiritualization
and not materialization came last. Jesus also promised that
if we seek first the Kingdom of God all other things shall
be added. That is the right order: Seek first the spiritual
and the eternal and then trust God to take care each day
of our physical needs. Certainly such praying if genuine will
never try to take the place of our proper responsibility. In
any case, asking refers to all needs, but creatures need more
than the spiritual to sustain them in this world.

In asking we acknowledge ourselves to be children in need
of love and creatures in need of food. Our temptation is to
be independent, self-sufficient, instead of ready to accept
our proper place in creation. God wants us to ask for our
sake. He wants us to learn that we are not central and beyond
need.

Children all too easily develop overdependence or a false
independence that breaks family ties. The way we ask God
shows the way we acknowledge him and accept his will. Asking registers the maturity of our spiritual life. We need
to pray, "Give us this day our daily bread."

In prayer we also identify ourselves with the will of God
for others. We share companionship with God himself as we
offer ourselves to help others. God does not violate human
freedom. He waits for willing human instruments. Asking
for others lifts us up to God by his grace and lets us come
down refreshed with power and insight to minister concretely to every human need.

I know no such joy and such spiritual power as when I
am allowed and enabled truly to pray for others. In such
prayer I can literally feel the surge of God's power through
my body. Such prayer never becomes a substitute for our
doing our part. It becomes an incentive to it and gives us
the power to do it the better.

One day when I was teaching at Mansfield College in Oxford, England, Dr. William Cadman, a distinguished biblical scholar there, told me that papyri had been found containing the Greek verb for "work out" as in "work out your own salvation." The Greek word came from working out gold from the mines. How right, I thought. God gives us the gold mines but we must work out the gold for ourselves. Without God's grace we can do nothing, but God's grace never takes the place of work.

But careful, now! If I don't watch out I am going to deny my original text. I may reduce the power of prayer to God's helping us to help others in some direct way. The text implies, on the other hand, that our prayers are taken right into heaven to be put into the golden bowls. Then they are poured on God's altar, consecrated to him, and returned with great power into the world. Prayer is no mere matter of autosuggestion or parapsychology. God does something far beyond using our small help. The Holy Spirit is not impotent to initiate and to carry through helpful action. Only faith in God's mighty works in human history is faith in true Christian prayer.

Our prayers are like a man signaling the sluicekeeper, who thereupon lets loose the mighty waters that float the ship and let it through the locks. We can't lift the ship by our efforts but by our willingness we can release the powers that lift it. We can signal for God's help. Such is true Christian prayer. We do not lift the loads of humanity by our effort. We have to do what we can; but even our best efforts are less effective action than they are like a mighty prayer that God will hallow his name by honoring our prayers. By offering up our freedom and our trust our prayers let God into the world.

We need to dare to pray with simple hearts, "Give us this day our daily bread, and forgive us our debts as we forgive our debtors." Not long ago my wife and three daughters were amused to hear me pray, "as we forgive our *daughters*"! Was I subconsciously thinking too much of our own power? True Christian prayer includes asking for God's help in every realm of need both for ourselves and for others.

IV

Prayer, finally, is affirmation. "For thine is the kingdom, and the power, and the glory, forever. Amen."

True Christian prayer is positive. It begins with the acknowledgment of God and ends by the affirming of his glory. Prayer when it is right becomes participation in God. The Holy Spirit prays in and through us. The words matter less and God matters more. We believe less and less in prayer and more and more in God. Therefore we naturally end by affirming the kingdom to be God's as well as the power and the glory. We have nothing and do nothing except in him, and in him we have all things and do all that is needed.

Jesus said that he of himself could do nothing. The very works which he did the Father worked in him. The more we become transparent to God's will the more we, too, shall know that prayer is participation, the more we shall know that it is God who works in us both to will and to do. The more we affirm the reality of God the more we become partakers of that reality. We pray mostly for God to become real in and for us. He alone is fully real; our lives become realized only in him.

Once we thought with Freud in terms of a small, helpless ego, squeezed between the imperious superego above and the libidinous id below. Illness was attributed to the repression of physical drives. Now psychologists like Mowrer of the University of Illinois, and others, are telling us that neuroses are attributable not so much to the repression of instinctive drives as to the repudiation of our moral strivings. We are made in God's image. On the Godward side that image is inviolate.

It does us no good to push our guilt into the subconscious. God's image is there, too. Unless we participate in God's will we shall go against the grain of our very natures. And we shall reap the consequences.

Many years ago I had a Model-T Ford that got in the way of a streetcar. I took it to a mechanic to have it repaired, and then I took it again and again, but something seemed always to be going wrong in that car. Finally the mechanic sympathetically advised me,

"Sell it for junk. When this car was hit, the chassis got out of alignment. The main line of the car is crooked, and as you keep on driving there is strain on it and something new is bound to snap."

That is our trouble, too. Our chassis is out of alignment and something keeps snapping. We lose our spiritual convictions. We get into moral mischief. We develop personality problems with others, or we become mentally oppressed ourselves. And often we develop all kinds of physical ailments without physical cause. We are out of alignment with God. Sooner or later something is bound to snap.

We need prayer. Prayer aligns us at the center of our lives with the will of God and opens for us the most effective way to become of help to others. But best of all in prayer God becomes real and life itself finds eternal meaningfulness. With full conviction I commend to you, I urge on you, a new life of true Christian prayer.

CHAPTER 4

Christmas Is God's Answer

The Word was made flesh. . . . JOHN 1:14

Christmas is God's answer to man's need for life and truth. We want and do not want that answer. We cannot stand the man with all the answers, and usually with good reason. Can we stand God's answer even if we were sure that it was his? If there is anything we do not want today it is to know the answers. Skepticism has always been endemic to academic life, but now skepticism is epidemic not only in our universities but throughout the entire intellectual community. We have spoken of how revelation grasps us; what grasps us *now* with all the intangible powers of our age is agnosticism. Once we admired honest and constructive faith; our ideal today is the honesty of the doubter and destroyer of faith, particularly if he deny the content of faith in the name of faith.

But there are moods when we are more receptive to faith's findings. A woman told me that in an ether dream she heard the answer to the riddle of the universe in a formula chanted rhythmically by an angel flying across the skies. A most reliable and thoroughly sane person, never given to credulity, she is steadfastly convinced that she heard the answer although she could not recall it upon waking. Christmas offers us peculiarly the mood of faith. It is no time for the argumentative mood any more than for the spirit of credulity. But it can give us the chance for honest openness beyond our ordinary routine of critical thinking. Within this unusual setting of openness, I want simply to suggest God's answer to our need for life and truth, within the kind of simplicity, in fact, that leaves both sincerity and sophistication behind.

I

In the fullness of time God answered man's quest for truth by a kind of life. We are accustomed to look for answers in terms of the results of experiments, the conclusion of logical arguments, the demonstrations of fact. God's answer in no way invalidates or calls into question such answers, but shows us that these contain but are not the truth. Man's most meaningful truth is neither of thought nor of fact, but is a way of living. The deepest understanding comes not at the end of an argument, but through the beginning of a new relationship.

Harvard's motto is *Veritas pro Christo et Ecclesia.* Modern man, embarrassed by piety, generally makes use of the first word only. But the motto is right in its deepest insistence that truth is for a kind of life and a kind of community, for the community of the kind of faith where peace comes through good will. "Glory to God in the highest, and on earth peace, good will toward men" is a most needed truth especially in this our dangerous day. The deepest truth for man comes not only within integrity, but within the integrity of the concerned life and the concerned community. The tragedy of Christmas is the obvious fact that we theologians and the Church in general have failed to make real and relevant the high truth of Christmas.

It is said that Emerson Hall, where many of us have labored, was intended to have around its frieze Protagoras' "Man is the measure of all things," but that President Charles William Eliot in the absence of the faculty during the summer had inscribed instead the deeper truth of Psalm 8, "What is man, that thou art mindful of him?" Both mottoes approach truth from the point of view of man, but the former cuts him loose from his ground and his goal. The life of Jesus is no isolated, chance happening of history. It is God's answer to our quest for truth.

During the days that I discussed the problems of philosophy personally with Professor Whitehead I was callow enough to ask him to define the nature of truth in one sentence. He surprised me. Truth means, he said, that life matters and has consequences. I asked him to elaborate. Life matters the most, he added, when we realize the most deeply that what we are and do has consequences for others.

God's answer to our quest for truth is a kind of life. Life cannot be compressed into a formula. It cannot be tested in a laboratory. We cannot establish controlled conditions for measuring life. Therefore God's truth cannot be externally controlled. But it can be tried. Jesus called truth a way and a life. He knew it from within himself. He asked us to become as children to know it, to shed our pretense, to rid ourselves of artificiality, to let go of our sophistication, and to enter into the way of concern and growth, of mature integrity, into the simplest yea and nay, into trusting acceptance beyond anxiety.

Much of Christmas for me is beautiful poetry, but I am increasingly persuaded that God's answer alone gives us the adequate reply to our quest for truth. Let us be thankful and responsibly serious about our findings of thought and fact. Such findings are the legitimate objects of our academic search. But the truth that can finally make us free lies on the personal level in a kind of life. Only by the finding of this kind of life shall Christmas for us have the kind of truth that gives fulfilling meaning to life and community.

II

God also answered man's deepest need by showing him his love. When we think of man's needs we often become guilty of defining them basically in animal terms. Man's basic needs, we say, are food, clothes, and shelter. And certainly man has need of these. On one level, man has needs in common with animals and it is good that these be met. But man is also more than an animal. His needs must be understood on his own level. Man is man. When God answered man's basic needs he gave him his love. Man does not live by bread alone. He needs bread, but even more he needs every word that proceeds from the mouth of God. That word is love. Man in the dimension of man lives basically by love. He lives at his deepest by meaning. He lives by the Word.

Such is the nature of our text. In the beginning was the Word and the Word was made flesh. And we beheld his glory as of the only begotten Son. Law came through Moses, but grace and truth came through Jesus Christ. The word of truth that became flesh was God's eternal Word of Love. This is the meaning of Christmas. This is the mystery of Christmas. A little child gazing at the living candles of the Christmastide has become wrapped up in the mysterious light of the Christmas story. The meaning can be put into words, but the mystery knows only the numinous silence that flickers in the darkness. Man's deepest need is to know the meaning of love, first in the circle of the bright light of a life of love, but also in the flickering mystery of the receding darkness.

Christmas is a pagan holiday if it celebrates only the turning of the day toward the natural light. The light of Christmas is the light of love which illumines the darkness of man's ignorance and sin. It is a light to lead us into the paths of peace. The Christmas symbol is built on no sign of language but on the life of love, fragile and frail amidst the world's darkness of evil. The bright meaning at the center thins out as the rays stray searchingly into the darkness of men's hearts.

We make a system of Christmas. We say the Christian faith celebrates a new kind of love, the fully open and inclusive concern. We compare this with other kinds of love and hold it to be theoretically superior. But God never gave us theology for an answer to our need. God gave us a life of love. He who came at Christmas told us of the kind of love of the father of the Prodigal Son, for the family; of the Good Samaritan, for the neighbor; and of the husbandman who paid each laborer according to his need, not his deserving, for political and social relations. He spoke in parables to keep love concrete and real. Even prayer itself depended for its efficacy on our willingness to forgive freely and to be freely forgiven. The kind of love Jesus taught never centered in character, but in concrete concern. Love for him was openness to human need everywhere, not as causes but through a fellow human feeling.

That love does not depend upon how we are treated. It centers always in the other person, in the community. It is a love, in Shakespeare's word (Sonnet CXVI), that never "alters when it alteration finds or bends with the remover to remove." Supposedly we celebrate this kind of love by the giving of gifts. The commercialism that besets such giving we can understand even though we cannot accept it. But Christmas giving is all too often a matter of wanting and getting. Or it is a matter of exchanging gifts. We give to those who give to us and write to those who write us. How different is the true Christmas spirit in its humble ministering to loneliness and need. It is good that we give on any level, but to understand and celebrate Christmas we must see love not as theology and not even as a moral practice, but as a life.

What characterized the life of Jesus was his self-giving. He gave of himself to people. He walked with those who were shut out by society. His best gifts were of his presence and of his power. Christmas never becomes alive in its true meaning until we see the Child in the light of the Cross. Concern for man beyond custom and convention, beyond orthodoxy and nationalism, led Jesus to the final self-giving. We celebrate Christmas as God's self-giving. That self-giving cannot be seen in its full meaning and mystery until we see the lonely, struggling man on the Cross. The joy of Christmas is not the joy of animal spirits nor of nature's turning, nor of any child mysticism. It is the joy of love's triumph in tragedy. Christmas was born not in Bethlehem but on Calvary. The star of Bethlehem shines only by the light from Golgotha.

We seek the fulfillment of life in being accepted, in being known, in being recognized, in quality of achievement, in attainment of security. As life matures and meaning mellows we see all such drives as the spoilers of peace. True satisfaction comes from the life of concern that is symbolized by Christmas. God met man's deepest need by giving us love. There can be no substitute for Christmas.

III

God answered man's deepest quest for truth by a kind of life and man's deepest need of life by showing his love. He also answered man's cry for salvation by coming himself. What this means is the heart of the Gospel. The kind of life we see in Jesus, the kind of love we meet in him, is the kind that identifies itself with others. To love is to identify oneself with the other. It is to cross the barriers and to bridge the gaps. God is no far-off absolute. He is no remote First Cause. He is no dominant principle. God is love who comes to us, not to condemn but to save. Well do we call Jesus Savior. His life is no abstract truth, no general love, but a particular love come to our rescue. In this kind of life, in this love, we find help. Here is our wholeness.

How differently God comes to us from those who are the world's great. He comes to us because he loves us. But he comes in utmost simplicity. He comes in breath-taking humility. He comes to us because he loves us. His coming is no paradox. It expresses his very nature. He waits for the right time to show us his full heart, a heart we can trust for doing right and far more than right for all from the beginning to the end. Here is the Source present in the process. Here are the Ground and Goal present in the temporal struggle. Here is the All-holy somehow present with man in all his sinfulness. God came to us and comes to us because he loves us. But he comes in us because he respects us. He comes not by the disclosing of his personality. What that means lies beyond all human ken. Only God knows God in the final dimension of truth and being. But he came in us as spirit. Spirit is flexible and feeble. He shares and partici- pates without domineering. The almighty God chooses to come as spiritual presence, waiting to be understood and ac- cepted. He comes inside us in order that he be present only to freedom, only to our true and real selves.

This is the mystery of Incarnation. Jesus was as human as anyone else. He was no God walking on earth and no semi- god entering history. He was man. God became man. The Word became flesh. The humble, holy God touched a life fulfillingly by his spirit in such a living way that when we see this life, when we see this love, we see conclusively clari- fied the central nature and purpose of God. God never forces his presence. He never coerces his children. He comes. One received him so fully that we call Christmas the fullness of time. Most men to whom he came received him not. But rather than longing to punish and kill the resister, Jesus suffered and died that the full quality of that life and that love might be made clear and become power by which we, too, can become the sons of God.

We think of salvation either as some pious word of the church or as some personal pious experience. But salvation is not external. God came to us because he loved us; he came in us because he respected us, because he wanted to safe- guard our integrity. Salvation is no escape from some ex- ternal hell nor admission to some place called heaven. Salva- tion is a matter of right relationship with God and our fellow men. Christmas means that God answers our need for salvation by offering us his own presence and power for genuineness and fullness of life. Surely near the Kingdom of God was the Muslim woman who prayed, "O God, if I serve thee for the fear of hell, burn me in hell; if I serve thee for the hope of heaven, deprive me of heaven; but if I seek thee for thyself alone, give me of that fulness." She knew the

inner meaning of Christmas. God's answer to our cry for
salvation is provided in terms of no external circumstance
but in terms of a kind of life, a kind of love, a kind of
relationship.

For human life and human love are not enough. They
flicker and fail, frail products of our created world. The only
Love strong enough to depend upon is the determiner of
destiny. Life, love, and salvation root not in human effort
but in divine reality. Unless man can look and long beyond
himself and find beyond himself the sources of his life, love,
and salvation, our hopes are meager and fugitive. Man has
a hard time to do with God but even a harder time to do
without him. Even those who shout God's meaninglessness
keep shouting about him. More and more I know the depth
of the mystery and stand awed before it, but less and less
do I trust human ingenuity and goodness to save us. Beyond
our puny might and poor wisdom with regard to ultimate
matters lies the endless ocean of God's mystery and might,
seen both simply and yet also unsearchably in Jesus Christ,
"the Son of his love." Somehow in that self-revelation of life
and love God has given his answer.

Christmas is no time to consider the problem of God. All
year we wrestle with that. Christmas is the time to ponder
the deeper mystery. If God is a problem for man, how much
more is man a problem for God. He has given us a kind
of answer that can give us life, love, and salvation. We know
that if in faith and commitment we lived integrity and universal concern, our problems as men would be potentially
solved. We know that such love casts out fear and makes for a
creative and fulfilling community. Why do we not hear and
heed that answer? Why, when at the depths of our lives we
know how to live, do we yet refuse to receive him who comes
to his own not to condemn but to save, not to judge but to
give abundant life?

Why worry about language at Christmas time? God's coming is "spatialization." Does the eternal literally become flesh?
The truth is simpler: Christmas gives us God's answer in a

kind of life we can trust, a kind of love that finds us, a kind of salvation that frees life. Christmas comes only to simple trust, be it of shepherds or of wise men, for God's answer is not an intellectual solution to be exhausted in systematic explication. It provides no *quod erat demonstrandum*. God's answer is an invitation to a kind of life, a kind of love, and a kind of salvation that involve humble, trusting acceptance of life. It is an invitation to pilgrimage, a walking in the way.

God came into a dark world with a strange light. The world is still dark and that light is still strange. But those who receive it even today receive the power to become sons of God, who understand the light in the darkness as they are born not of blood nor of the will of the flesh, nor of the will of man, but of God. As inner love gives newness of life, the Christmas light trembles with the fairest radiance life affords, and out of the darkness there still come voices in the night, singing,

"Glory to God in the highest, and on earth peace, good will toward men." "For unto you is born this day . . . a Saviour, which is Christ the Lord."

CHAPTER 5

All Things New for the New Year

Behold, I make all things new. REVELATION 21:5

Well, here we are, starting another year! What will this year mean to us when all will be over and we face God? How new will be our lives, our minds, our spirits?

The problem with life and history is that things do not become new. There is at least an almost despairing sense in which both personal life and human history stay the same.

This is true of personal life. How much most of us have to own this fact to be stubbornly real. Some fifteen years ago I heard Reinhold Niebuhr tell a gathering of theological students that growing old, even for a Christian, did not mean growing out of problems, but that we would remain much as we were. Many of us were shocked by what seemed a clear and outright denial of God's promises that we may grow in grace. But those of us who now have reached the age that he was then have to admit that he spoke more truth than we knew.

Reporting about his year as president of British Methodism in the *Methodist Recorder,* Leslie Weatherhead avers that one reason for lack of relevance and effectiveness in the pulpit is that ministers preach the ideal of the Gospel and not their own experience of it. If they preached what they knew, they would no longer discourage the laymen by the false implication that while the laymen failed to find glorious and constant victories of faith in their personal lives, the ministers did so.

Instead, said Dr. Weatherhead, the ministers should tell the truth of their mental and spiritual failures and doubts,

their sins and their sorrows. This article was so real and so
vivid as to be another testimony to the fact that, even for so
great a man as Weatherhead, things do not become new
just because we grow old, even in Christian service. How
many are there who, knowing themselves, dare to give contrary witness?

This failure to become new in the sense of permanently
better also affects social life. Has our century solved its problems? In what real sense has there been a radical solution
of our total problems as a civilization? Are we not living in
the century of the whirlwind? Read Pitirim Sorokin's treatment of the history of war in the fourth volume of his *Social
and Cultural Dynamics*.

Are family patterns more satisfactory and family bonds
more solid? Is mental illness on the decrease in our culture?
We need hardly broach the subject without finding the
answer. Perhaps, moreover, this century can be called the
century of the sword of Damocles as well as the century of
the whirlwind. There is such fear of the future that, as *Time*
says in a survey of American life, to mention the danger to
civilization from nuclear weapons is to be guilty of bad taste.

Things do not become new, for one thing, because there
is no controllable way of accumulating moral and spiritual
gains. Intellectual gains can at least be preserved in books
and on records, to become vital to any age, although even
these gains have to be appropriated. Moral and spiritual
status, however, is mainly a matter of decision over and over
again.

Witness, for instance, the decline of denominations. A
small group of people become galvanized by a new spiritual
insight and for it they sacrifice and live until they become
veritable dynamos of spiritual power. The next generation
partakes of the drive and vision. After a while, however,
those who have profited from the drive often become comfortable in mediocre ways and well adjusted to the world as
it is. The zeal is gone, the power stops, the experience dies.
Within the shell of an institution, life maintains itself, but

the glory and the spiritual growth are mostly past. So also civilizations flourish and decline. Who can look at the history of the world and say that in this world things become new?

In spite of the facts of experience and history that things do not become new in the radical sense proposed, our hope is still in the openness of life and of history. Under God history is of our own making. *History is flexible to faith.*

Life is like steering. As persons we get pretty much where we want to go. Not, of course, that we can control the conditions of life. They are mostly given to us. We are born with good minds or poor, crippled or well. But the meaning and power of life are equal not to our given circumstance, but to what we do with that circumstance.

One of the most tragic verses of the Bible is from Psalms (106:15): "He gave them their request; but sent leanness into their soul." The people of Israel could even change their situation, but the result was still not according to expectation. How many people have gotten to where their pride has driven them only to find that what they obtained was not what they had expected or wanted?

On the other hand, remember those who turned unfortunate circumstance into victory. Jesus sought to help the world and the world rewarded him with a cross. But a reward it was, for he got what he wanted, the result of a love that cared unto death. What an amazing success story also on the part of the saints, a story of martyrdom and of victory; for when love is the aim, the victim of hate becomes the victor!

For persons, therefore, life is open. It is a matter of steering. Our hope lies in the openness of life.

History, too, is open, a response to challenge. The British Commonwealth has been facing its "economic Dunkirk." Following the war it was asked to fight the new battle of Britain on the economic front. The truth is that Britain could slip back into a tragic has-been. Such a slump is all too easy. But in spite of hard circumstances, Germany has been coming back. So can Britain. In the realm of the mind, in the realm of atomic industry, in the realm of international leadership, history is open to those who can.

In every realm the limits of history seem to be up and down, *but not forward*. History exists for decisions, for learning freedom and co-operation. Therefore we cannot eliminate problems from history without destroying its purpose. We need never worry about heaven ever taking the place of history. In history we never shall be ready for heaven.

Our hope is real, however, for life and history are open even to the past. All that is real of the past is in the present. All yesterdays are in today. And they are in today subject to change. They are living parts of it. Any choice we make today, therefore, changes also the past.

Jokingly, I tell my students to distinguish between the "wasness" of the was, and the "isness" of the was. The past as past is dead and gone. The past as living is vitally present for our choices. Thus even the past is ours to redo. The past, instead of being a burden, can become a great aid to the present when it is understood, accepted, and used. It is a river that comes with power into the present, which, rightly directed, can help us change an unsatisfactory present for a better future.

The glory of our hope is that life and history are open, that we can respond to challenge, and that all things, at least potentially, can be made new. Our decisions under God are the key to the making new of life and history.

Our hope is in the openness of life and of history, but our faith is in God. God is Lord of all. He is not of history, but before and beyond it.

There is now some return to supernaturalism. Whatever words are used, Barth has led a revolt against all mere religions and against any Christian faith centering in the natural order. God simply is no mere part of process, however important to it or in it. God is the creator of the ends of the earth, the controller of all histories and the completer of all that his hand has made.

On the Continent the problem of transcendence is being waged with fury. Emil Brunner says that Karl Barth's irrelevant objectivism resulted in Rudolf Bultmann's impotent subjectivism. Be that as it may, my own conviction is that we shall find again a relevant and powerful supernaturalism centering in the Incarnation. History, I believe, is now heading home.

There is also return to mystery. The Christian faith has within it mystery. Only mystery can give depth to faith. Mystery sometimes results in a glorying in irrationalism and in paradox as the essence of faith. Far from it! Paradox is our creation. It is either the result of sin, hiding the truth, or of our looking ahead where every new step must be a paradox because the ladder of revelation is never raised from the earth, but hangs down from heaven. The discontinuous "not yet" must be a paradox until its unveiling.

Mystery in the Christian faith is, rather, revealed truth too bright for us to encompass except in part for present purposes. No one stressed paradox more passionately than Sören Kierkegaard, but he knew that in itself Christianity was, as he said, "complete certainty" and "crystal clarity." From within the revelation, for the spiritual man, there is light and not darkness, but a revelation that is so wondrous as to be called by nothing so much as mystery.

When St. Paul reaches his fullest vision that God has consigned all to disobedience, in order to have mercy upon all, he needs must cry, "O the depth of the riches both of the wisdom and the knowledge of God! how unsearchable are his judgments, and his ways past finding out!" (Rom. 11:33).

God has ordained history and work in it. Christ is its center. While God is sovereignly its ruler, he is yet available in love to all who call upon him. History is determined because God is sovereign. Yet history is free because God is love. Our freedom is real, but within the final purpose and power of God.

Cybernetics—the comparative study of the human nervous system and of complex electronic calculating machines, with

the object of increasing the understanding of how the human
brain functions—shows us how a target can be reached even
though the object pursued, like a fleeing ship, is free to
change its course. God is no mechanism, but greater incomparably than any mechanism! He knows both how to make
us and our freedom and how to use them for his boundless
love and for our total good. The Ground of history is its
Goal.

The consummation of history is God's work! When all is
related to his purpose, "Nothing walks with aimless feet."
In a field theory of freedom there is no determinism of mere
strains and stresses, for the parts play their part, but neither
is any initiative anywhere unrelated to the power exercised
by the total field. Similarly our freedom counts and is needed;
but it is, nevertheless, within the field of God's activity and
control. God who began creation will finish it, and not by
any arbitrary fiat, at that, but in a way fully consistent with
his declared love in Jesus Christ. It is within such a great
history that we are now working. It is within that wondrous
activity that we begin this year.

When I was a boy in Sweden, I walked five miles to school
every school day. As I turned the first corner and left behind
the last building of our place, heading for Gnesta, where
the school was, I used to say, mostly to myself, "I'm almost
there now." Starting is important, and starting in the right
direction with plenty of strength is more important. Christ's
love for all within faith's strength in God is the right direction and gives us the needed strength.

With God there is always power to spare. My God is able
to do more than we can ask or think and he will answer our
needs according to his riches in glory in Christ Jesus. Christ
is with us through the Holy Spirit to the end of the world. In
Christ we start the year. Within his power we start aright.

CHAPTER 6

The True Christ

. . . to speak the mystery of Christ. . . . COLOSSIANS 4:3

With our present return to serious theology the question who Christ is may be the most vexing and critical problem of today. There are two basic ways of looking at Christ. They involve basic differences as to our understanding of the character of God, the person and work of Christ, and the nature of man himself. This sermon aims at clarifying the heart of the Gospel.

According to one view, which I reject as unchristian, God is self-sufficient Being. It follows from this point of view that God did not need to create, that God is not by *nature* Creator. God in himself, as trinity, is perfect community. Although it is wrong to worship three Gods, God is never solitary. The Godhood contains community. God has no need to create in order to be or to know community.

Whatever else can be meant by the trinity, the doctrine, within the context of God as self-sufficient Being, affirms that God does not need to create community. Such a being cannot be known by us, as he is in himself, but only as he has declared himself to be in the Bible, in Christ, and perhaps in the church and its traditions.

Speculative thinking about God is therefore always antifactual. How he is, he has disclosed sufficiently for our salvation. To reason from such revelation in order to obtain more information is to miss the truth, since it is impossible to go from the category of man to the category of God.

From the claim (which I repudiate) that God is self-sufficient Being, it follows also that God did not need to come down to redeem man. Man's fall is not God's fault. It is due either to man's deliberate disobedience that forfeited his status as a child of God or to God's eternal will to create some vessels to honor and some to dishonor. In either case man has no right to judge God. God alone is judge and the sovereign determiner of destiny.

Luther writes that God did not need to come and be made man, but rather was it needful and profitable for us.

Calvin's view of God, in respect to grace beyond justice for some, has been fairly compared to the case of Negro prisoners in a Southern state. All guilty, they were allowed to pass in review before the wife of the governor who, according to an established custom, would pick some for pardon who could thereupon serve in the governor's mansion for a year before being set free.

Similarly, it is held that all men are guilty before God. The fact that some are saved by his mercy cannot be held against God's justice, but only contribute to the praise of his mercy. For man to judge God, according to this first view, is pride and vanity. God is eternally and sovereignly self-sufficient Being beyond any need to save man.

It follows further from this erroneous position that God not only did not need to come to man in order to save him but does not need ever to fulfill human history. God did not need to create in the first place. God is not *by nature* Creator. Nor did God need to enter world history to save man. God is not *by nature* Redeemer. But neither does he need to fulfill human lives or history at any final time. God is not *by nature* the Fulfiller of history. God is self-sufficient Being who will never be bothered by the eternal death or suffering of the creatures. That is simply not his affair.

God will finish human history, continues this position, in his way, the way of the sovereign will. His business is to uphold perfect righteousness. He is inviolably holy. The fact that the Bible tells us that only a part of the world will be saved illustrates the perfect, nonsentimental justice of God whose ways are not man's ways and whose weaknesses are not man's.

God did, in fact, create; he chose in love to come to us in his Son; at the end, according to this view, he will judge some to righteousness and some to damnation. Man's duty is to worship and to love God, the self-sufficient Being who is final truth, right, and standard of love.

According to the second main view of Christ, which is insistently my own, God is not self-sufficient *Being*, but self-sufficient *Love*. In creating, God performed no arbitrary act. He did not remain in bliss through half eternity, if so we may speak, and then decide in the midst of eternity to express his bliss by doing the one new thing for him, creating. To create, rather, according to our second point of view, is no new experience for God. It is no external act.

Creating is, rather, part of the nature of God. It is a way in which he who is Love expresses himself. God creates precisely because he is outgoing creative Love. Thus loves God. He loves nothing as arbitrary or as external to himself, but loves his creation in loving himself and loving within himself.

God needs to create, not as a lack of being, but as the perfection of love. God needs to create as a true mother needs to love the child. Such need is no failure but the authentic revelation of motherhood. The nature of infinite love is to create the finite, to redeem its freedom and to perfect it.

The trinity, in this view, stands necessarily for the fact that God is not self-sufficient Being but an outgoing Love who comes to create, to save, and to fulfill. We know this God because he has revealed himself in the fullness of time, as the fullness of time, in Jesus Christ. The Bible tells the story of Jesus Christ and the story of all men in the light of God's presence as literally holy Love, inclusively and unconditionally, in Jesus Christ.

Such a self-sufficient Love who creates out of the perfection of his nature also redeems man out of his own perfection. To love is to identify oneself with the beloved. To identify oneself with the needy is to care for them and to help them. To identify oneself with the sinful is to enter into their plight and deliver them from sin.

One of the themes I want to repeat through life is that
God came *to* man because he loved man. He came *in* man
because he respected man. He who is Love knows that love
cannot be given as a package but only as a person. Man's
freedom must be kept inviolate, letting man find for himself the Love for whom he was made and accept and mature
in this Love. Therefore God himself came, to identify himself with us, to enter our plight, to do on our behalf what we
could not do for ourselves, namely, to open up acceptance
from his own side that we might find the forgiveness of our
sins and free fellowship within his Love.

Calvary was promised in creation. God's suffering and con-
quest of sin, of law, and of death by his resurrection over all
of them were part of his eternal purpose in Christ precisely
because he is the God we meet in Christ—the God who is
self-sufficient Love.

Such a God who creates and redeems because he is Love
also fulfills man's history because he is Love. To create is to
prepare for fulfillment, to redeem is to effect conditions for
fulfillment, to be God is to fulfill to perfection his own
work. Because God is Love, creation matters. Because God is
Love, God cares eternally and comes to save us. Because
God is Love, God seeks the last child more surely than the
good shepherd his hundredth sheep.

Until the children find heaven and home, God sorrows
and longs; he seeks and woos; but at last he seeks and finds.
He has made the far country a place where his wayward sons
ultimately starve and are in want until they come to themselves and return. Thus loves God, because he is not self-
sufficient Being, but self-sufficient Love.

II

There is not only a basic divergence as to the view of God
in these two ways of looking at Christ and of following him;
there are also basic differences as to God's relation to man in
Christ. According to the first, which I reject, Christ is and

works mainly as God in a human body; according to the second, Christ is and works mainly as God in a human being. In either case the key is the presence and power of God, but in the former case the key is the presence and power of God acting through a human organism; in the latter case, the key is the presence and power of God acting through a human personality.

In the first view, which I consider theologically harmful, specifically, Christ became Man, but never *a* man. He took on human nature generally, but never became a human personality specifically. Jesus is eternal, the second Person in the trinity. He was born of Mary directly by God and grew a body through which to communicate with the world and to work the redemption of man on the Cross and by rising from the grave. In the cradle lies, consciously and omnipotently, the King of kings. The eternal Son clothed in flesh passed through time, through human history, revealing the Father and affecting man's redemption by his suffering and resurrection.

Therefore, Christ, in this view, suffered as God, not as man, except as a happenstance of co-suffering. Only the infinite can pay the infinite debt, even though he takes human form for the rendering of the payment. Jesus died as God and raised himself as God. The deathless that cannot die, dies, and, as deathless, cannot be held by death, but conquers it.

Consequently, *in this distorted view, Jesus was never fallible*. He was born perfect by the generation of the Holy Spirit in the Virgin's womb and never lacked the power and reality of perfection. He had to be free from sin through his whole life, from beginning to end, because God cannot sin. He knew all things all the time because he was God and, therefore, again, his every word is literally a word of God infallibly given for our salvation. Jesus was never free to sin, to fall, to fail in any respect because he was God.

This is no caricature of the position *in its main intention and contention*. Various ways are taken to account for, but mostly to ignore, whatever in the New Testament goes contrary to this main affirmation that Jesus was eternally, and from birth to death, infallibly and sovereignly God. Jesus Christ is Lord and Savior, because he is God, and this and this alone is the meat and matter of the Gospel.

According *to the second main point of view, however,* which to me is triumphantly Christian, *Christ's work is basically performed as man. God acts in and through a genuine human being.* God became man. The Word became flesh. Jesus was a man. He is no mythical man, but a real, historic, human being. The most important fact about him, of course, is not his humanity, however high and however new, but God's presence in him. The Gospel of Jesus Christ is summarized in our meeting God in man and in what God did for us through man.

Yet the whole purpose of Incarnation is the humanity of Jesus. God sent no external message nor did he come as a man different from other men, but came as true man, as a real human being. He came thus in order that he might be real and relevant to our lives. He entered our ordinary nature to enable us to become rightly related to God, which is the essence of salvation.

Accordingly Jesus suffered as finite man. He suffered as one born and brought up under the law within the conflicts of the flesh. He knew personal problems, for to this end God identified himself with us. Jesus was tempted, suffered and died as a man, but as a man with such presence and power of God in him that God became revealed and operative in human history through him.

With deep discernment Luther has written, "Thus making a happy exchange with us, he took upon him our sinful person, and gave unto us his innocent and victorious person, with which we are now clothed and freed from the curse of the law."

A favorite hymn of my father has it that we must exchange hearts with our Savior. Vincent Taylor, a prominent British New Testament scholar, tells us that Jesus became *our representative,* acting on our behalf or on our account. The humanity of the Son of God is the medium by which the historic Jesus actually becomes Mediator.

Jesus had to know and to assume our failures, our mistakes, our limitations, and our sins in order to conquer them. God "made him to be sin for us, who knew no sin, that we might be made the righteousness of God in him" (II Cor. 5:21).

Long ago Gregory of Nazianzus said that what was not assumed was not healed. In Jesus God as Son assumed our total alienation from him and made a living way for us to him precisely through his flesh.

God, obviously, cannot sin. Neither can the Son of God sin, as God. The power of the Sinless can alone conquer sin for us. And sin was conquered in Jesus by the victory of his Life, the Cross and Resurrection, but it was conquered because in him sin had come to do its best to tempt and to overthrow the Son of God, but was routed in the struggle and was dragged to the Cross to be killed.

In this same victorious humanity we may partake by accepting within ourselves the eternal Son of God. The Son of God, God's outgoing Spirit, is the head of humanity; in our humanity we can also find victory as Sons of God whenever our sins are nailed to the Cross of God's complete self-giving for us and raised with Jesus to newness of life.

The point is that God became organically and fulfillingly present in a human being, Jesus, beyond any mere human body, reconciling the world unto himself and raising Jesus from the dead. The nature and purpose of God are thus seen in the person and work of Christ Jesus, the Godman, the first-born from the dead in order that he might have many brethren.

III

The two different ways of looking at Christ entail divergent views of man as well. In the perspective that assumes God to be self-sufficient Being, and not self-sufficient Love, man is thought of as basically a guilty sinner. God gave him his freedom. Deliberately he sinned. Thereby he forfeited all right to claims on God. Man's only relation to God now is therefore one of guilt. For God to do nothing but to punish man is merely to be true to his nature of perfect purity and inviolable justice. In this sense man is totally depraved, deserving either eternal death or eternal punishment.

There is, in every case, no good in man to earn God's acceptance and no faith in man to avail himself of God's work. If man is outside the protecting grace of the work of Christ, he is by nature a lost sinner and *nothing else*. In this view there is no necessary, inner relation between God and man. Man has forfeited his chance to be saved and his destruction or damnation in no way affects the inner life of God. God is only carrying out his will for a rebellious realm to which he is not related by any inner, lasting ties of duty or of love.

In the case where God is conceived of as self-sufficient Love, however, through his being and working in Jesus as the Christ, man, on the contrary, is conceived quite differently as a potential Godman, a potential saint, or a potentially new creature in Christ. This is the glorious Gospel of the New Testament. Chalcedon, the true confession that Jesus was fully God and man, is normative psychology as well. Man becomes mature only when he comes into right relation with God. How realistic the Christian faith! How relevant!

From this second point of view Jesus showed us both God and man. Augustine wanted to know two things only: the nature of God and of the soul. In Jesus these two questions are answered. Because God created as Love man is from the beginning a creature of Love. Man is by origin the child of God as Love.

God is Love and man is made in his image by Love for Love. Man's basic relation all the time, furthermore, is his relation to God. The basic thing about man is not that he is a sinner. He *is* one. The basic thing is rather that, sinner or no, he stands in relation to a Love who made him and who calls him into fellowship with himself and with all who are made of God. Man is made to be won by God.

Potential man, not actual man, is proper man. God's ultimate will for man is more real and true than man's present will for himself.

God's freedom to be God and have his own way, even in love's freedom, is incomparably more determinative than man's right to rebellion and his actual rebellion, through which he is to find himself and to find God's way to be best. A God-centered and Christ-centered view of man is thus more important and more real than a man-centered view. Man is a sinner. There is no denying the fact. But more significantly, he is made by God, stands in relation to God, and is made for God.

As a matter of fact, as we have already suggested, man is made to have God in him. Even as Jesus, because God was conclusively in him, became the first full man, even so we become fully human only as we realize our own true and full potential to be rightly related to God. Jesus was the first Godman in the crucial sense of the word. We are called by God in him to become Godmen. We are called to have the Word in us, to have Christ in us as the hope of glory, to have the Spirit of Christ in us. To be a new creature in Christ is not merely to have our original creation restored; far from it!

With Christ came a new age. The end of all things which is true beginning came with him. The Kingdom of God came with him. God as Love, in the proper sense, came with him, fulfilling, correcting, transforming all else. Incarnation, God in man, is no isolated instance in Jesus, but the purpose of all creation. The eternal purpose of God was realized in Christ.

The Creator became crucified for our sake; and he who is least in the Kingdom of the crucified and risen Creator is qualitatively greater than the greatest of all prophets of law and justice. Jesus humbled himself all the way to the death on the Cross wherefore God gave him the name above all names, the name of sovereign Lord as saving Love.

The more Christ lives in us, the less we, too, become in ourselves. But when we are thus losing our lives, we find them, until we all become filled with all the fullness of God. We become members of the body of Christ whose fullness fills all in all.

The humanity of Jesus is crucially important because it is the door into our humanity, it is the pledge for our humanity, it is the victory of God for our humanity. The same Son who once came for our salvation in the true humanity of Jesus now comes in us as Christ the hope of glory for the world. Thus we are joint heirs with Jesus Christ, sharing in our lives the same God and the same humanity.

All men, furthermore, belong within Christ potentially, for God is bound to them with cords of love that can neither break nor wear out. God as eternal Love will not rest satisfied until the children of his love accept his love. God sorrows for the lost. He identifies himself with them in suffering and sin. He works to save them.

The very nature of the body of Christ, the true church, is to be a community of continual concern for the world. The fact that God cannot be satisfied without all his children is no lack in him; it is the perfection of Love, signified by the fact that even if we are faithless God remains faithful (for he cannot deny himself), and sealed by his sacrifice in death for us.

Thus you and I are worth beyond all objective descriptions because we are the objects of God's creative and redemptive concern.

We have given a few hints as to the nature and importance of two divergent views of Christ. One starts with God as self-sufficient *Being* and backs this view with biblical quotations, to the effect that God is not intrinsically nor eternally related to the world in terms of responsible and effective Love. The other view starts with Jesus Christ in terms of the Love that he himself demonstrated and taught, arriving at a view of God as self-sufficient *Love*.

The choice between the two is critical as to the character of God, the meaning of Christ, and human nature and destiny.

My own deepest conviction is that we cannot halt on both sides. Our ultimate view of God, consciously and far more unconsciously, determines our cultural patterns, our economic and social life, our racial behavior, and our national and international relations.

The Christian Gospel of God's universal Love in Christ comes as our fullest judgment as well as our greatest hope. One or the other is right. Choose we must and do.

My own choice is committedly that God has come in Christ not as self-sufficient Being but as holy, self-sufficient Love. I believe that we as Christians shall see a day of full power in personal living, in community, in thought and action, in worship and work, only when we repent of our faithlessness and by faith and grace accept, live, and proclaim the whole Gospel of a whole Christ for a whole world.

CHAPTER 7

The Way, the Truth, and the Life

. . . I am the way, the truth, and the life . . . JOHN 14:6

Many of us have come to believe that Christ is the way, the truth, and the life. What, however, do we mean by this familiar statement? Does it mean something that really matters? To be sure, I do not wish to put too much stress on the meaning that we can understand, for life always outruns our understanding. There is a genuine mystery about life that every healthy and mature person experiences. The measure of intellectual adequacy, says Alfred North Whitehead, is our sense of mystery. Not ignorance but the ignorance of ignorance is the death of knowledge.

Nevertheless, Christ is far more than a symbol of life's profound mystery which we must accept. He is also the symbol of life's meaning. He is the disclosure to man of the way and will of God. The very center of mystery radiates saving truth. How, then, are we to think of Christ as the way, the truth, and the life?

I

Let us consider Christ as the way of integrity. Jesus lived and taught that our eye must be single if we are to see truth. If the eye is not single the whole body becomes filled with darkness. Jesus hated sham. He dared to say even of Moses, "He said . . . but I say unto you"! Jesus knew that the tree must be made good if it is to have good fruit. His chief enemy was hypocrisy. To walk in the way of Christ is to accept the way of his integrity.

Personal integrity comes hard. We have so little of it. Suppose we were to be given Glaucon's ring, which Plato wrote about. If we wore it we should become completely invisible and get away with whatever we wanted to. What should we do under such circumstances? We mostly play a role. We do what is expected of us. We are mostly hopeless conformists. Deep down we question whether what we say or do is true or right, but it is not healthy to behave or to think differently from other people if we are to be generally accepted.

A professor on a university campus said that although he was a church leader he believed nothing at all of the Christian faith. He claimed that he had discussed the question with many leading laymen of his city and found that 75 per cent of them shared his unbelief. Yet he did not want to disillusion his child and his students by telling them the truth! Do you have similar feelings?

Glenn Clark used to tell the story of how at a ranch in the Rockies he got the handsomest horse he could find for a steep mountain climb. But he had to go the long way around because the horse had worked so long in the city that it had lost its ability to track. When the hind hoof fails to hit exactly where the front hoof struck, the animal is no longer safe on a narrow mountain path where a slip means death.

Even so we have lost tracking power between our conscious and unconscious minds. We have lied so long to ourselves that we cannot tell what integrity means. When we yield to the pleasure principle and do what comes easiest rather than what is right, the mind goes to work to hide from us what we have done.

The mind goes about to keep the self whole. If the conscience causes deep enough conflicts, and if the self genuinely repents, the mind can keep reporting the truth. But if the self persists in its false way, the mind begins to distort reality in order to keep us together as a personality.

By long practice the mind gets so used to distorting the world for us that we see everything in false shape. There-

fore "the reality feel" is nearly all lost. Conscience is largely
silenced. Convictions for the real, the right, and the good
grow feeble.

Freud saw this fact and thought he solved the problem
it gives us. The ego he found to be helpless between the
superego (the conscience) and the id (the pleasure drive).
By explaining away conscience as false authority the self
could find freedom within the life of the id.

The Christian knows that only a false conscience can be
explained away. Some psychiatrists are now saying that it
is not the suppression of the instinctive life, but the suppression of conscience that causes neuroses.

The only way to be made whole, to be integrated, is to
accept Christ as right conscience, or universal love, in terms
of which we can repent, be forgiven, and be restored to reality. Christ is the way of personal integrity, of facing reality
which is the way and will of God.

How true is this need for integrity in the social realm! We
live in an age of disintegration. Chancellor James Hamp-
ton Kirkland of Vanderbilt University is reported to have
said long ago that we are at least two hundred years on
the way to destruction. Symptoms are too many to mention.
When the police department must alert high school teachers
to be on the watch for large-scale narcotics consumption,
spreading from individual to individual, when small cities
report a million-dollar-a-year loss from shoplifting, when
public laws are glaringly flouted by both makers and en-
forcers of the law, we need not more than mention the
obvious state of general corruption. Society needs the way of
integrity.

Part of our problem is the valueless clutter and the wealth
of history. We swallow both and have indigestion. This is
true even with respect to our historic faith.

Let me illustrate. A guru in India could not keep his cat
from coming in and licking the milk on the altar. During
each worship period, therefore, he tied it to the door of
the tent. After some time the guru died and eventually so

did the cat. Thereupon the people could not worship until they had tied a cat to the door!

We need a resolute cleansing of our faith if we are to live richly by what is everlastingly true in it. We have too many cats tied to our doors.

But more important is the need for intellectual honesty that does not shy away from tackling the thankless task of intellectual, social, and spiritual leadership.

I believe the churches may be more responsible for dishonesty than any other institution, where people week after week repeat what they may not fully believe and actually seldom intend. Usually we find it convenient to accept instead of the full and saving truth the mixed truth that not only cannot save but that, too diluted with death, leads to death. We must work on the way of integrity in social morality generally. Within a community concerned for truth and general welfare new incentives to integrity must be born. We want to be made whole. May we never forget that integrity is the price of integration. Christ is the way to integrity. We need the light of his austere honesty thrown on our motives and lives.

II

Jesus is not only the way. He is the truth. I have spoken of the way of integrity by which alone we walk toward God. Jesus is also the truth of love. God is love and Jesus is the Son of his love. What do I mean by the truth of love?

First of all, I mean that truth cannot be had apart from love. The loveless are blind. They are blinded by their own sin. This is quite the opposite of the usual notion that love is blind. Love is blind only when it is selfish love, and that is no love.

Sentimental infatuation refuses to see the full truth. It sees only what it wants to see. No one is so blind as he who does not want to see. But such infatuation is not love.

But what of the fact that a surgeon does not operate on a

member of his own family lest his love undo the steadiness of his hand or make him shrink from doing what needs to be done? It is not the love that a surgeon has that undoes him, but the self-involvement that gives rise to anxiety. Perfect love casts out fear.

In the realm of personal relations we are blinded to the objective truth by our likes and dislikes. For many years, probably because of an unfortunate childhood association, I found it difficult to like or to trust anyone who wore a particular kind of pince-nez spectacles that happily for me has gone out of style. Social groups, too, see things from the point of view of their own interests. Such distortion of truth is no deliberate act. It is no conscious attempt.

Reason is like the lamp on a miner's cap that sits squarely in the middle of our forehead. It throws light on whatever way we turn. When we want to see things our own way, reason obliges us faster than we can sense its distortion. We are convinced that what we see is the truth.

The truth of love is the truth of faith and hope. It is the facing of reality. Only those who trust God dare to face fully the truth of this world, including the challenge of true hope. The rest despair. Only those who have walked the way of trusting concern will dare to open their eyes fully to the hurts of self and of the world.

For love's truth is no easy truth. It sees how we all seek our own self-aggrandizement. It sees more and more our lack of integrity. It sees the plight the world is in and grieves.

Faith and hope see with Jesus' eyes the people as having no shepherd and the nation as blind to the time of its peace. It weeps not only over Jerusalem but over Washington, London, Peiping, and Moscow. Love dares to take up the cross of caring because the truth that we find by love, we find because we have first been loved by Jesus with God's great love.

Love's truth is the truth that God is far from us and not real to us until we find him on a cross. The immense spaces and the moral law give no adequate answer to the God of a world like ours. Only the God who hangs on the Cross can answer the depths of human suffering.

If God so loves the world—the God who made it and who governs it—surely we human beings can have faith and hope. Him we can love.

It is a fact that truth is in proportion to our suffering. A psychiatric counselor from New York has said that we live in proportion to our having suffered. Reality comes by means of our crosses. Whom God loves he also chastens, the Bible proclaims.

All talk of a theology of success is cheap. Our faith is in the Cross. All talk of power through positive thinking is cheap if God's positive way of the Cross is set aside.

The Christian faith does not make a good out of man's desire. It knows that God's way is the Cross and that the Cross spells out concretely the truth of love. We find our lives only by losing them. In taking up our crosses we meet the Master.

When God's complete self-giving is met by man's, then and then alone does it become clear why our eyes can be opened only by love and why we then see both ourselves in need of forgiveness and restoration, and a world in need of new crosses for its light and healing.

Take a look back at history and watch the rise and decline of original Christianity. Only the church that believes in the necessity of vicarious suffering understands the redemptive task of the Christian community: to live not for itself but for the world at the expense of self. Why is the world repudiating Christianity? Because of its shallowness. Our young people are deserting in droves not the Christianity of the Cross but the Christianity of conformity.

III

But, after all, the Christian faith is not a dirge but a paean of joy. It is a Gospel from God. The way of integrity is therefore no way of mental flagellation. The truth of love does not end on a cross. The Gospel's last word is life.

Those who walk in the way of integrity find life. Those who know the truth of love find life. They find thereby the only life which is life indeed. They discover the abundant life, and life more abundantly. They find life everlasting.

Alfred North Whitehead made fullness of life the final criterion: to live, and then to live in an ever more satisfactory way. Neither was he an optimist. To him God was the sufferer who understands, man's companion on the way of integrity and within the truth of love.

Certainly life itself is no boon. It is not enough just to live. Witness our suicide rate. Then ponder the number of those who never dare take that plunge, but who are steadily unhappy. One of the world's great religions makes escape from life its chief and final good. The more we come to know world weariness the more attractive it may appear to settle for some escape from the burdens of existence.

But Christianity offers not merely life but everlasting life, and everlasting life not simply as duration but as the kind of life that is worth living eternally. This kind of life cannot be found by study. It cannot be achieved by work. It is the gift of God's love in Christ. The gift demands sheer acceptance within the love of God.

Study should enrich such life. Work should follow. But only as we accept the Way of Christ, God's own gift of love, can we find the truth that sets us free for real life, for the life that is worth persisting worlds without end.

The more I see of life the more convinced I am that most of us never find it. We never learn to live. We chase life rather than live it. The simplest need is the hardest to fill. How to fill it is hidden from the wise and the mighty, for neither wisdom nor might can discover it. It flees from force and cannot be taken by violence.

It is the simplest truth of accepting all of life in God and living with joy and peace in believing because the God of hope has made us to abound in hope. How unreal Paul's phrases sound to modern man! Life's deepest know-how is knowing how to have our minds cleansed by faith as we walk on the way of Christian freedom. It is allowing the love of God to be shed abroad in our hearts through the Holy Spirit.

Strange words are these to all strangers to such experience. This is equally out of the reach of both modern sophisticates and classical pagans. But such life can be had by each and all who will walk in the way of complete integrity and learn the truth of love—the free gift of God.

Life in Christ makes us real. Christ is the real kind of life, the life of genuine love. This love makes us genuine. It makes us authentic, and it lasts. Eternal life cannot be spelled out. We cannot know what mortal thought cannot grasp and what human tongue cannot tell.

But this life is as sure as God himself. God is not like the Greek god Kronos who steadily devours his own children. To believe that of the Christian God is to blaspheme. He fulfills, not destroys, life. Time is not God, but his creature. Wise is he who now finds eternal life. This life is over before we can grasp its flow. A poem the authorship of which I am unable to trace runs something like this:

> My newborn infant tumbles from my arms
>   And trudges off to school;
> A youth walks home with her; their child
>   Brings me a shawl and stool.

So brief is life. So long is eternity.

When Christians forget that we are pilgrims and strangers to this life our neglect shears Samson's hair. The strength of the Christian faith lies in its knowledge of life everlasting.

Those can live well above human opinion and personal pain who know the triumph of life eternal. They know in the midst of earthly life the joy which can abound in the midst of affliction. They know that the Cross is fulfilled by the Resurrection. Because they already know life eternal they face the present with confidence. Because even in this life they know the power of an endless life they face the future without fear. Those who know real life, life in the Son, life as sons of God, know that Christ as life is the way and the truth.

Many voices call us to follow. The promises are luscious. The temptations are alluring. Life can be lost by indecision. Before we know it our life is gone and we have lived frustrated rather than fulfilled.

Christ calls us into his way of truth and of life. As we follow him we have to admit with Peter: "To whom shall we go? Thou hast the words of eternal life" (John 6:68).

CHAPTER **8**

The Three Witnesses

There are three witnesses, the Spirit, the water, and the blood; and these three agree. I JOHN 5:8

The Bible should be allowed to state its own case as to our knowledge of God. There is a biblical model for organizing, evaluating, and directing experience. We need to polish this biblical model in order to deal more authentically with the religious problems of experience.

Science uses models. Models help to disclose and to clarify what science studies. Such action may seem to deal with the abstract rather than with the concrete, but knowledge of the concrete comes most effectively by such a method. Long ago Bacon criticized Copernicus because Copernicus seemed to him to be dealing with mathematical formulas rather than with the actual observation of the rotations of the heavenly bodies. But in effect Copernicus answered that he believed his mathematical model and that time would prove him correct. It did!

In our day Lord Samuel, a British scientist, has taken Einstein to task for trusting mathematical models more than the immediately available physical data. The infinitely large and the infinitely small are hard data to handle! In a famous letter Einstein replied that creativity belongs to mathematics and that he trusted his model. Within the proper scope of truth I believe time will prove him correct as well.

Similarly we need to polish our biblical model with which to illumine general experience. We think we are being both more honest and more adequate when we stick close to the facts of experience. But experience is what we need to clarify

and change. We need the right model for doing both. I
believe the Bible provides us with that model and that we
must use it with conviction and with whatever competence
God has given us.

I

Our text instructs us that there are three biblical witnesses
to the reality of God's revelation. There are three to testify
to us concerning our right knowledge of God. These are
the Spirit, the water, and the blood.

Incidentally, for the sophisticated, my sermon aims to pull
together, within the power of the Bible, the three strongest
drives in modern theology. In expounding the Spirit as a
witness I shall deal basically with the claim by Neo-orthodoxy that revelation is self-authenticating; in connection
with the water I shall treat Neo-liberalism's stress on God's
presence in history and nature; and in discussing the blood
I shall try to express the truth of Neo-evangelicalism's stress
on the grace of God through Christ our Lord.

The first biblical witness is the Spirit. The New Testament
itself reveals the primacy of the Spirit as witness. It proclaims boldly, in the verse before our text, that "the Spirit
is the witness, because the Spirit is the truth." The Spirit
is no witness merely to God's presence. It *is* God's personal
presence in the believer and in the Church. Kierkegaard
ridicules anyone who tries to prove someone real who is personally present. Such an attempt insults the person!

It is now widely rumored that in the third volume of his
Systematic Theology, Paul Tillich will formulate his whole
approach to history and eschatology in terms of Spirit. If he
succeeds at that task he will surely help us. The Spirit is the
truth, and Spinoza pointed out that the truth is the criterion
both of itself and of error. The truth is its own best witness.

Nietzsche startled many by declaring that God is dead. He
also accused the first person who defined God as Spirit of
having killed him. God is dead for modern man precisely

for the opposite reason. Modern man does not know the reality of the spiritual category. Therefore he cannot know God. "God is a Spirit; and they that worship him must worship him in Spirit and in truth" (John 4:24).

The Bible says God is Spirit. St. Paul announces boldly that if we do not have the Spirit of Christ we are not his. We cannot belong to him. We cannot participate in the life God is. Therefore we cannot, of course, know God. Spiritual knowledge is basically by participation.

Nicodemus came to Jesus by night. He represented the learned in Israel. He belonged to its ruling class. When he could not understand Jesus, Jesus chided him for being a ruler in Israel and not understanding the presuppositional nature of Spirit. Unless we are born again, born anew, born from above and by the Spirit, we cannot know the kingdom of God. How many leaders within our churches are equally blind to the elementary facts of the Christian faith? Our model says that the Spirit is the truth. How many really know from within the reality and working of the Spirit?

The flesh avails nothing; the physical by itself is no good; the words that Jesus speaks to me, he stresses, are Spirit and life. How many try to know God by human wisdom and in terms of ordinary secular knowledge! It cannot be done. We must become living spirits, touched, transformed, and made to see God by the quickening Spirit who came in Christ.

The Spirit, then, is the truth and we know the truth only by being born of it. We must participate in it. We come to know God not only by belonging to the truth and being within the truth. We come to know God also by the power of the Spirit. When we abide in Christ the Spirit frees us to know the truth even as the truth then also sets us free.

The natural man, the New Testament warns, does not understand the words of God's truth. They are spiritually known. Before St. Paul made that declaration Jesus had mystified the Pharisees by asking them how they could possibly think that they understood his words when they did not receive his Word. The words (lalia) Jesus used found meaning and life only within the context and the reality of the Word made flesh *(logos)*. The words expand and fill in the details of the Word but cannot be understood, much less appropriated, except as part of the Word of God. How we fail to stress that the Gospel must be spiritually understood!

Both Berdyaev and Kierkegaard knew that the nature of inwardness is Spirit. The spirit of man is the free center of man. But man's freedom goes astray and is futile and frustrating apart from its infilling by the Holy Spirit as the main witness to the presence and power of God. The Spirit must witness with our spirit that we are children of God. Only the Spirit can give us the click of conviction that God is real and is for our best.

John Wesley, in his mature spiritual wisdom, taught that spiritual experience is to faith what physical experience is to reason. Without physical experience we human beings cannot think at all. Kant called reason without sense empty. Just so we cannot have faith if we are empty of spiritual experience. Apart from the experience of the power of the Holy Spirit in our lives our faith is empty of God. And a vacuum is soon filled with other things.

My admired professor of theology, Daniel Evans, once preached a sermon on God. After the sermon a shoe manufacturer whom Dr. Evans knew well came up to him and objected,

"I don't know any God. I don't know what you are talking about. Why don't you talk common sense?"

"Bill," responded Professor Evans, "what do you think about the first thing in the morning: shoes?"

"Well, that's my business, and of course I get ready for the day."

Continued Dr. Evans, "Then during the day you keep on with your business? You think all day of shoes?"

"I suppose so."

"Then at night," Dr. Evans persevered, "you often, no doubt, go out with business associates and your conversations stray off on shoes?"

"We shouldn't, but I guess we do talk shop all too often."

"Bill," said Dr. Evans, "the trouble with you is that your mind has turned into a last. You cannot know God by a last!"

Such is the sad truth for all too many of us. We do not live in the Spirit, we do not walk in the Spirit, we do not think in the Spirit, and obviously we cannot know God in the Spirit. God is Spirit. The Spirit is the truth. We know the Spirit only by the power of the Spirit. We cannot know God except it be given us by the power of the Spirit. We need his presence for God to become real.

The biblical model also insists that the Spirit is the secret of spiritual communication. The Apostles spoke as the Spirit gave them utterance. They moved to preach where the Spirit directed them. They were restrained from going certain places by the guidance of the Holy Spirit. The Holy Spirit is the secret behind the mighty works of God called the Acts of the Apostles.

What does Pentecost really mean but the power to communicate in unknown tongues? Pentecost means the miracle of communication beyond external barriers of nation and language. It means speaking in the tongues of the hearers, getting across to them in spite of seemingly impossible obstacles. Pentecost is the miracle of the ears as well as the miracle of the tongues. Pentecost is the miracle of communication.

Today we worry about the problem of communication. We study techniques. We try tricks. We blame the absence of community for the failure of communication. Our main problem, however, is still the human problem of original sin. Religious proclamation and religious reception are jammed by man's sinfulness. He refuses to hear. He turns off his spiritual receiving set. He tunes in on secular channels.

The Holy Spirit when he speaks in us creates community. He engenders the conditions for spiritual hearing. He communicates. He breaks in on all wave lengths. He cannot be kept away by jamming. Man, hearing him, can suffer and refuse to heed. But they must hear. Too long have we tried tricks. Now we must stop speaking in words and techniques that man's wisdom teaches. Once again we must speak below the level of man's conscious evasion of the Gospel to address the depths of man by the demonstration of the Spirit and of power.

Kierkegaard tried a neat trick, the indirect method of communication. The Bible itself illustrates this method. When David had sinned, for instance, the prophet Nathan did not confront him directly with his sin. He did not tell the king that it was wrong for a king with many wives to take away the one wife of his trusted soldier. Instead the prophet told the story of a rich man with a hundred sheep who treated his guests to the one lamb of his neighbor, the dear little lamb that slept and ate in the neighbor's bosom. When David flew into a fury at such outrageous behavior, the prophet turned the knife into David too late for him to defend himself: "Thou art the man!"

Indirect communication has its place. The Bible itself for us is mostly God's indirect confrontation of our sinful and needy lives. But there will be no conviction and conversion apart from the power of the Spirit. At the depths of life man is related to God. This is the dimension of depth in experience. God is there to meet man when he comes most deeply to himself. We shall, of course, not win the world for Christ apart from the power of the Holy Spirit, but neither shall we win anyone deeply to himself until he comes to know himself as spirit and becomes rightly related to God and to all men within the Spirit.

Thus the biblical model is clear and convincing. God is Spirit and the Spirit is the truth. God's self-revelation in Christ as holy love can be known effectively only within the reality of the Spirit. The Spirit must live in us. He alone gives power of conviction in our knowledge of God and he alone gives power of communication of the Gospel.

If you want to know God, stop trying human wisdom and turn to God the Spirit. Open your life as spirit to the Holy

Spirit and God shall be to you reality and rest, he shall become your security and your strength, he shall be for you
meaning in life and fulfillment.

II

The biblical model for Christian truth claims that the
Spirit is the truth; therefore it is primarily its own witness;
the deepest spiritual truth is self-authenticating; but the
water and the blood are also witnesses, not to themselves,
but to the Spirit, to God, to God's work in Christ. In this
respect Neo-orthodoxy is right in its claim that revelation is
self-authenticating; but the Neo-liberals are also right when
they claim that creation and history witness to God. To be
sure, nature and history cannot prove God. They cannot
give the believer the inner conviction. Only the Spirit can
do that, but they can speak their own language in their own
measure, witnessing to the reality and power of the living
God.

The water stands for creation. To be sure, the narrower
exegesis is baptism. But the rite of baptism is the witness
through a material symbol. It is the witness to the creature,
needing the physical expression of the faith. The Spirit is
the truth and is self-sufficient once it is fully attained. But
until such attainment the creature needs the material means
of witness.

The water in the Bible often, at least, stands for creation.
In the beginning the Spirit hovered over the waters. The
Covenant of Noah concerning creation is a water covenant.
Jesus is baptized with the Spirit upon his baptism in water.
I asked an Old Testament professor about this exegesis. His
informal reply was that he had specialized on this question,
and assured me that if I was never right in any other
exegesis I need have no fear for this one! All I can claim is
that this interpretation makes this passage peculiarly meaningful as a biblical model.

Creation witnesses because the history of creation is the

history of revelation. The renowned scientist, Teilhard de Chardin, in *The Phenomenon of Man* astonishes me by his approach to the *within* of matter. Plurality, unity, and energy are the three phases of matter that have been commonly accepted. But these cannot be understood in their power to develop our astonishing history of creation unless we grasp the fact that always there has been an unseen side to matter. There has been the *within*. The history of evolution is the history of the revelation of the meaning and power that have been unseen from the beginning. Evolution has conspired in its utter majesty and mystery toward our present attainment because of an inner reality that has become externalized in matter and the whole history of creation. The history of creation has been the history of revelation tending toward the Omega point of God's presence and purpose.

In any case it seems altogether likely that even in secular thought we are about to break through the incredibly naïve ideology of the nineteenth century that believed in evolution from below: In biology Darwin was the main formulator; in history it was Marx; in psychology it was Freud; but all shared the assumption that this utterly complicated creation of ours came about through development from below without adequate cause or purpose. And hardheaded men in hardheaded universities, as they thought, fell prey to such naïve ideology and taught it as fact.

A hundred years after Darwin and more we are just beginning to outgrow such immaturity of faith and to face the facts. The mystery may deepen before more light will break, but in the end Darwin's century will be put in its place of both honor and limitation. I believe that our conception of God will have to grow beyond present imagination, but the more we come to understand the biblical model aright the more we shall also find that the best interpretation of creation will witness to the reality of creation as the work of God. The history of creation will stand out as the history of revelation.

The water, or creation, also witnesses through the voice of history. The voice of nature speaks a duller note; the voice of history speaks a fuller note. To be sure, the problem of the interpretation of history is persistently difficult. But real beginnings toward fuller adequacy are being made. A new journal, *History and Theory,* in its first issue had an exceedingly important treatment of the subject by Sir Isaiah Berlin, a professor of social theory at Oxford.

A professor of history at Harvard drew a few of us together to discuss the relation of religion to history. He had started, he told us, as mostly a positivistic historian dealing only with facts. Then he had come to realize that interpretation of history implied some kind of philosophy. But philosophy, he said, snips off the ends of interpretation, and that night he was looking for a theology of history.

The problems of historic interpretation are legion, but beyond details of interpretation there can be piercing shafts of light thrown on the main meaning of man's history.

Man has been driven by his needs and his meeting of those needs from an isolated food-hunting animal, or groups of such food hunters, to a citizen potentially of one world. Technological invention, that is, has sired relentlessly sociological and political extension in man's kind of community. Man, so to speak, has been caught in the push of this process. He has been driven from behind by his needs. To meet these needs he has been forced by history to face wider and wider modes of community.

At every stage of this push of process, however, man has had to discover the pull of purpose in terms of which life becomes livable in a satisfactory and constructive manner. Man has not only been pushed from behind; he has at the same time been drawn from ahead. He has been both driven by need and lured by ideal ways of living. Human history is a constant deciding how to accept the pull of purpose with regard to the push of process. Man finds the push; he chooses the pull.

This pull has two criteria: an open society, or else there

are destructive conflicts or walled-off stagnation within man's community; and an inclusive society, or else there is deadly conflict and destruction among societies.

All the time man has had to decide between his push from behind and this pull from above or ahead of him. For every kind of community there is a relevant way of living. The way man has decided between God's push in process and his pull of purpose has determined the course of human history.

The fully open and inclusive society was glimpsed in Jesus Christ. He is the fullness of time. He is fullness of meaning. He is the standard of human community. Tillich calls him the unique, nonrecurring Kairos, the final way time should be filled. Bultmann calls him the once-for-all expression of authentic existence in human history. In Christ there is neither Greek nor Jew, bond nor free, male nor female, black nor white, capitalist nor communist, for all human beings find their dimension of depth in him.

We cannot know all the answers to human history; we can only snatch at its meanings; but in Jesus Christ we see God's answer to the needs of human history and the power for meeting those needs. Therefore we preach Jesus Christ as God's way of salvation for all men. We join with Peter Taylor Forsyth in affirming that although we cannot know all the answers we can know the Answerer. That is our final faith.

The water also witnesses in that our historic decision for the future demands spiritual reality and power.

In the long past man's whole way of life was revolutionized when he learned to use tools. Tools are the indefinite extension of man's hand. Would man be man without his hands? Consider how man can manipulate his world because of his having a thumb. Would man be civilized in any advanced sense apart from his technology?

The present revolution in man's life, more than we know, is surely the indefinite extension of man's brain by means of automation. The entire tempo of man's life will be revolutionized because the cybernetic devices can calculate in micro-seconds problems that would take mathematicians months to solve. The symbol of this revolution is man's reaching out into outer space for probing and power. Who can guess what our children's children will know and do?

But man's hand threatens to destroy us and man's brain can prove the truth of orthodifferentiation, namely, that in evolution the species is destroyed by its very overdevelopment. A distinguished medical man from South America assured me that he believed that man had eventually to destroy himself by his brain according to this law! To control man's long hand and to direct man's extended brain, therefore, we need spiritual resources. We need constructive meaning for life and the power to avail ourselves of such meaning. The third great revolution in man's life needs, therefore, to be the extension of his spirit into the reality of the Spirit. Our basic need now is spiritual vision and power.

Education without ends now spells ending without fulfillment. We must know and teach the reality of true values. Our central task now is the spiritual. The Church needs to be revolutionized to know that the fundamental revolution must needs come now in man's heart. Realism now calls for a truer relation to God the Spirit.

III

The Spirit witnesses as the truth; it is the truth. The Holy Spirit can witness only to God the Spirit, to himself in human history; but the water witnesses insofar as creation and history bear faithful testimony to the truth of the Gospel. The Christian faith is no false pietism and no learned speculation; it is the sheer realism of human history and human life in the light of God. But there is also the third biblical witness: the blood. The blood witnesses to the Spirit.

Some people object to hearing about the blood. They forget that it is a central biblical truth, and that the Bible does not use anemic language. Superficial liberalism has objected to a wooden literalism. We want to go beyond both. Neither groveling in gruesome theology nor running away from realism into sweetness and light can help us.

Biblical realism affirms that God as Spirit becomes redemptively involved with the world. He is always there as the creative power. Creation continues. But he comes to creation with redemption. He comes to the water with the blood. And the water and the blood agree.

The biblical model by the testimony of the blood witnesses to the reality of the Cross. Love's identification with the world unto death on the Cross witnesses to God. It was prompted by his presence. We tend to shrink from suffering. Love becomes one with the sufferer to bear his burden.

The biblical model of the blood affirms that all theologies that teach that God abstains from the world's sufferings and evils are heretical. It will have no truck with the philosopher's unmoved Mover. The height, absolutely the height, of human horror is the picture of God and the saints making eternally merry in heaven at the expense of an eternally tortured humanity. These lost creatures did not ask to be born. Some theologians have even had the saints look down on the people in hell the more truly to praise God for their own salvation. Such theology is man's vilest thought and needs utter redemption.

The witness of the blood, on the contrary, is to the effect that God cares enough to come to the very depths of human sin, to enter into man's worst sorrow, to take on and overcome man's most devastating failure. The Spirit needs the witness of the blood. It opens our eyes to the central fact that God has the faithful character of unlimited and universal concern.

The blood testifies, also, to the fact that we see God in those who are constructively self-giving. What else makes Jesus Savior? When we think of those who have been Christlike, do not names like Schweitzer, Kagawa, St. Francis leap to our minds? Even non-Christians, technically, like Gandhi and Socrates, speak to us of the eternal Christ in human history. We know through their lives that God did not limit his incoming to his conclusive coming in Jesus. Because of the witness of the blood we call Jesus Lord and Savior and by that testimony we know that all true identification with the world's needs in suffering and joy are Christ's because Christ is God's.

When we come to our own deepest experiences of God, too, we know that they came in such experiences. The Spirit witnesses to us through the blood. We know God through our crucifixion of selfish ambition and the shouldering of the concern of others.

Once when I first moved into the South, I woke up around two o'clock in the morning hearing a large crowd moving relentlessly toward my campus home. The day before, I had entertained a Negro friend over the warnings of some of my colleagues. The confused din, the loud voices, the clinking of metal convinced me that I was about to be lynched! My whole body stiffened, like a stone slab, and up and down my spine went hot electric currents of agony. And yet my spirit sang. "Thank you, Father; thank you, Father," my heart whispered. If I had been murdered then, God would have been indescribably real and near. But instead, the commotion turned out to be only a fraternity initiation, and I was safe to keep witnessing. God came to me in this suffering, in the identification with the cause of humanity.

Another time that God came unbelievably close and comforting was when, after hours of struggling with myself and the issues involved with regard to my participation in World War II which had just come to America in the Pearl Harbor attack, I finally decided as a Christian leader that I had to oppose war and preach peace. I then thought that conscientious objectors would be imprisoned, and perhaps even shot. I believed the war would get worse and worse and that those who refused to yield to the war spirit would eventually be liquidated. My worst inward fight concerned my own family. I did not want to leave my wife and several small children unsupported. But when I finally decided for God's will, as I knew it in my spirit, peace unbelievable and the presence of God flooded my life. We receive God's testimony to our sonship in the witness of blood.

Therefore we must preach Christ and him crucified. We have no other Gospel as Christian preachers than the message of the Cross. God came to us to save us by the blood. How can we understand so grand a truth! How can we communicate so great a salvation! The witness of the blood is the witness of God's work of redemption in human history, centering in Christ but gathering up and fulfilling every intention and act of concerned commitment. The witness of the Cross is finally the witness of God as love, a love that not only cares but can. Therefore communication concerning God, our preaching of the Gospel, must center in the Cross, the witness of the blood.

Thus we have tried to expound the meaning of our text. The Spirit witnesses as the truth. It *is* the truth. It is self-authenticating. Nothing else can prove the Spirit. The Spirit uses means and signs to its reality and work, but these cannot prove, only witness to the truth of the Spirit. We can know God only as we are born by the Spirit and receive the witness of the Spirit to our spirit that we are the children of God.

The creation, however, is a needed witness to the work of God. The water bears its own kind of testimony. Barth used to deny this part of the biblical revelation which the liberals never ceased stressing. Now Barth, seeing the centrality still of the confessional approach of the Spirit, also repents of his inadequacy at this point and wants to remedy his lack in future works. We need a combination of witness at this point that is fully biblical. The Spirit *is* the truth and the water witnesses *to* the truth.

But we must never forget the witness of the blood. Confession and self-authentication are not enough. We are not basically concerned with revelation but with salvation. Nor can we confine preaching to philosophy and science. God's presence in creation and history as a whole cannot give us a clear and full-saving gospel. We need the preaching of the blood. We need the witness of the Cross. Christianity ceases to be Christian when it stops being evangelical.

Beyond science and philosophy, yes, beyond every theology, but including their fullest truth, lies the reality of the full Gospel according to the biblical model. We must polish this biblical model and confront men with it, for this is God's message to man's deepest need and to his inmost heart.

"There are three witnesses, the Spirit, the water, and the blood; and these three agree."

CHAPTER 9

I Am Sure

. . . I am sure that he who began a good work in you will bring it to completion. . . . PHILIPPIANS 1:6

Poor Paul! He must have been either very insecure or else frozen stiff in his own past! At least it is the claim of some psychologists that at whatever point we are ourselves the most insecure, we make the loudest and strongest claims in order to assure ourselves that we really do believe what we say.

The preacher, accordingly, will pound the pulpit when he is the least sure of what he is saying. He is really trying to convince himself, you know, that what he is saying is true and that the role he is playing is right. Notice that Paul appropriately added, "It is right for me to feel thus." Was Paul himself perhaps uncertain precisely that he who had begun a good work in the Philippians could actually bring it to completion? Did he make himself say, subconsciously, in order to subdue his misgivings, "I am sure"?

Or Paul might have used such an emphatic statement, "I am sure," exactly because he had closed his life at this point. Students of the science of cybernetics remind us that living is a matter of steering. It is a matter of continually adjusting our past within an ongoing present by means of decisions for the future.

Just as the magnetic torpedo in pursuit of a ship readjusts its course whenever the ship changes its course to avoid the torpedo, so we must likewise continually readjust our own lives in the pursuit of new goals. New experiences should enrich life and broaden the scope of truth. To set the rudder of life once and for all is to miss the adventure of the voyage and to lose sight of the larger goals.

So persons, churches, and civilizations can become frozen stiff in these areas. To be dogmatic is to suffer from a frozen decision. Poor Paul said, "I am sure," when perhaps he should have said, "Right now it seems to me rather likely that. . . ."

Or perhaps he had earned the right to say, "I am sure." Perhaps he actually was sure. His certainty, in any case, to a large extent changed the course of human history. Let us grant that insecurity and dogmatism are always ready tempters to an immature and an unearned certainty. But let us consider well whether there cannot be the kind of certainty that stems precisely from security, from insight, from open-mindedness, and from obedient maturity.

Such certainty, in any case, is never based on external authority, be it church, creed, or book. However much these may guide us toward the sources of certainty, they cannot give certainty. External authority is the acceptance of some-one else's say-so. This acceptance evidences immaturity. It is precritical; childish, not childlike.

People believe the Bible, the *Koran,* the *Sudras* or *Vedas, Science and Health,* the *Book of Mormon,* the Westminster Confession, *Das Kapital,* or the prevalent scientific or philo-sophic dogma with the same naïveté. In this precritical stage they themselves simply accept without seeing. Consequently, they dread doubt and resent having their faith questioned. No wonder that they are inwardly insecure, defensive, or dogmatic. In any case, they are immature.

I remember how desperately I myself fought in this pre-critical stage to retain my own faith in the verbal inspiration of the Bible. My long battle ended in humiliating defeat as I sank to my bedside, crying, "If there be any truth any-where, help me at least to be honest in finding it, and to know what I believe and why." Physical pain I have known inti-mately and long, but what a far more horrid experience to have one's intellectual and spiritual umbilical cord cut off completely. Such pain is itself nevertheless a witness to the primacy of the meaning of life. Most people suffer in their subconscious, little knowing what real life is, depressed by the fear that no real purpose can be found.

There is, however, another kind of certainty which is usually not accounted as such. This is the certainty of the critical. Have you not known people to say, "I am sure that no ultimate truth can be known by man"? With what certainty those in the critical stage will argue that one can know with certainty only analytical truth and sense knowledge only as probable.

Really such certainty is based on insecurity and immaturity. An evidence for this, I think, is the hurt delight which some of those who have come into their critical period take in convincing others that their certainties are false. Their own denials must be confirmed by others, and for this reason they work hard and long to persuade others that they can be sure that all human knowledge is relative at its heart, that religion is nonsense, that the power of the Gospel is merely an emotional state. Or else some people in the critical period smile with a sophisticated condescension at the certainty of the believer, thereby assuring themselves, of course, to be more sure, more near the truth.

But those who have passed through the precritical and the critical periods and have truly entered into postcritical maturity know far better what Paul meant when he said, "I am sure." They know because they have seen; they know because they have experienced; they know because they go from light to light within the power of the Holy Spirit.

Paul could say, "I am sure," because he had witnessed God's mighty acts in history. The Gospel of Christ was not mere academic speculation. Though Paul knew not Jesus in the flesh, he knew him in living experience. The life of Jesus was no mere theory; it was power to heal spirit, mind, and body, a life of abounding inner peace and freedom, a new kind of community, leveling the artificiality of human barriers and creating open, adventuresome human relations.

God's act in the Christ-deed was the power of his own love, beyond human origination and control. Paul lived within the burst of that new power unto salvation, made real and ready in history, which made him unashamed to say, "I am sure," because of what he had seen.

Paul could also say, "I am sure," because he had personal insight into the meaning of God's mighty deeds. These events for Paul explained experience and the course of history. Not only had his physical eyes been opened, but so had his intellectual ones. He had been cured of more than his psychic blindness; he had gained his spiritual sight. Do you recall his majestic interpretation of the drama of history in the Epistle to the Romans? Do you hear his anthem of insight into the nature of love in the First Epistle to the Corinthians? How experience is lighted up by the reading of the Epistle to the Philippians! Only they who have worshiped the Lord God with all their mind in surrender of defensive pride and with critical honesty can give a reason for their faith at their level of experience and earn the right to say, "I am sure that God. . . ."

How often I have walked and walked in search of a faith more real and true. After each experience I have come back even more convinced that I am sure that I see what God has done and what this means for all of us frail and sinful people, who are nevertheless sovereignly created for God and for the community of his perfecting.

An old riddle tells of a man who was found hanging in a room locked from within but on a rope too high for him to have reached by himself, with no furniture in the room on which he might have stood. The question is, "Was it murder or suicide?" When the solving clue pierces the mind—dampness on the floor indicates that the victim had stood on a large cake of ice which subsequently melted away—one is struck hard by the possibility of the solution.

Much more is one struck by the force of meaning of Christian truth to solve life's problems, when one really comes to see. As A. E. Taylor has said, "Knowledge is vision." Paul had more than the vision on the Damascus road. He had the vision of what Christ meant for the world. Therefore he could say, "I am sure."

Paul could also say, "I am sure," because he had himself experienced Christ. He had himself been delivered from the dread of the law, for Paul, as for Martin Luther later, God's great achievement was in Christ. He had been freed from the power of death and died daily. How he faced stonings, floggings, persecutions—all for the love of Christ! In prison he could exclaim, "For me to live is Christ, and to die is gain."

How he had experienced the power of forgiveness whereby he could cry, "Abba, Father," even while sin worked in him! He had been raised with Christ and had set his mind on things above until he could exclaim, "Who shall separate us from the love of Christ?" Paul lived in the present, because his past was forgiven and the future was in the hands of God. He would not mind earthly things, thereby becoming an enemy of the Cross of Christ; for his conduct was in heaven.

There is no substitute for personal experience. The mind can be convinced without the whole self feeling sure. Mere intellectual vision is sterile and unsatisfying. Laymen, clergymen, missionaries, even famous professors of divinity have spoken with me, disturbed for lack of conviction in spite of the fact that their minds were convinced of the truth of the Christian faith. Paul could say, "I am sure," because his whole self had experienced the power of the Gospel. Hence he could say, "I am sure that. . . ." His convictions were no mere logical conclusions, but continually confirmed existential commitments.

But when all is said and done, Paul could most readily say, "I am sure," because the Holy Spirit witnessed with his spirit that God can finish that which he has begun, and this witness was the inspired experience of going from light to light.

The Holy Spirit tolerates no closed system; he keeps leading us into all truth. The infinite Creator eternally evades being exhausted by his creature. The Spirit breaks through all human finalities. Where the Spirit is, there is life as adventuresome steering and no rigid rudder. Where the Spirit is, there can be no defensive dogmatism but a humble open-mindedness. It combines with God's own certainty to produce divine assurance within us. There is no frozen decision of life, but a going from light to light as we obtain light within the living Word of God.

God's truth is definite without being specific. A child can trust his parents' love and feel definite about it without knowing specifically how that love will express itself. He can also be free to gain maturity, as the parents' love allows him serious choices according to his state of development. So God's love is definite without being specific, bestowing upon us the grace of freedom, riskful choice, and the chance for real maturing.

The Holy Spirit is never a pampering parent nor a sentimental nursemaid, sparing us the risk and adventure of steering. While he provides no closed external authority, he does, of course, use the fixed stars of his own revealing, and the lasting landmarks of God's mighty work in history. But certainty comes only as we go from light to light, as we keep steering toward the distant, unfolding goal.

As we know the certainty within, the Spirit witnessing with our Spirit, and as, outside, we see progress in the journey, we can say with an increasing and relaxed assurance, "I am sure."

When the Holy Spirit witnesses with our spirit, and when our lives are fulfilled within the will of God, then we become possessed with a certainty which needs neither external defense nor internal justification. Though we know in part, we nevertheless know that we know and, more importantly, we are fully known.

This world is looking for certainty to make it free and secure. Certainty can be had, but only at the price of doing God's will. Within that will are quietness and confidence.

Within that will are peace and power. Within that will are both rest and creative satisfaction.

As we live ourselves into it and are lived by God, false certainties and false uncertainties alike begin to fall away and we earn the right to say with Paul, "I am sure." ". . . I am sure that he who began a good work in you will bring it to completion. . . ."

CHAPTER 10
Not of Men

Paul, an apostle (not of men, neither by man, but by Jesus Christ, and God the Father, who raised him from the dead); and all the brethren which are with me. . . . . GALATIANS 1:1-2

Christians should be the convincing reality of civilization. They should be the creative minority that gives coherence to community, that makes our life not only tolerable but creative and rich. The modern ministry, to help the church be strong, needs the full apostolic power of the Gospel. Now what makes a minister an apostle? First of all—not of men, not what comes from man. Not of men.

No one ever becomes a minister by *ability*. God gives the ability. But by no ability in the world, by no measure of ability whether we have 95 I.Q. or 195, are we going to be made ministers of Christ. As a matter of fact, it is said that not many wise or learned are called.

This fact has changed so that William G. Pollard, internationally famous scientist at the Oak Ridge Institute of Nuclear Studies, told me not long ago that the most brilliant people are now going into the ministry. Well, that's not going to hurt it, but I don't think it's going to help it either. Not by itself anyway.

Yes, it's not by ability, although we'd better use our ability to the fullest. Nor is it by *works*. That's of men, too!

I had a professor of theology who got up at four-thirty in the morning, was in his study at five, and worked until twelve o'clock every noon. And he "went places," as we say. But I am sure that he never became a *minister* by hard work. I believe that men *should* work, had better work, and many

99

of us don't work hard enough, but no one is ever going to be a minister of Jesus Christ by work. Paul, an apostle—not of men.

Nor can a person be a minister by *personality*. There are a lot of men who use their personalities—they are good handshakers, they can get along pretty well—as a matter of fact I had a letter from a church—it was one of these suburban churches; it was a "country club" church. And the letter read something like this: "Dear Dr. Ferré: We are a church that has no problems at all. We are a very wealthy, suburban church. Our people come from the best families. We are looking for a minister. The only qualification is that he have a good personality—that he be personally acceptable in this sense."

And I wrote back: "Dear————: I am very happy in these days to hear about a church that has no problems. My own experience is that country club churches are usually spiritual slums. 'How hardly shall they that have riches enter into the kingdom of God!' Therefore. . . ."

Not by personality—there are lots of people who are getting along on their personalities. We need a good personality. As a matter of fact, Phillips Brooks defines preaching briefly as truth through personality. But no one is ever going to be a preacher—no one is ever going to be a *minister* by means of his personality.

In the second place, if it isn't by men, what is it by? *Men? by man?* It's not by *families*. It's not by family background. I'm not going to stop on this, except to thank God for the kind of family background many of us have had. The kind of background of people who knew their God.

But no family can send us into the ministry. I've been listening to a person that I should like to see go into the ministry and I know how his family is praying that he will go into the ministry. He comes from a very fine family. But no one can go into the ministry in terms of his family.

Nor by *education*. This is not the place to say too much about it because some of us are involved, but I know that we

try to give people a balance between the theoretical knowledge, the historical knowledge, and the practical knowledge,
and send them out with a message for a world like this. But
no one is ever going to become a minister *by his education.*

Nor by his *position.* The way ministers sometimes work to
get a better position you'd think they'd be nearer the Kingdom of God if they were in a better church. And the way it is
often put is that we need a sounding board. You see, we have
a voice, and the position we have is supposed to be a sounding board. And if we could only get the right kind of
sounding board, the Message would spread out and spread
out.

The peculiar thing is that God needs no sounding board.
When the Holy Spirit speaks, he creates his own sounding
board. Jesus didn't have a sounding board, coming from
Nazareth. I can go through history and show that many great
people didn't have sounding boards. But God talked through
them.

No, not *of* men, nor *by* man, but *by Jesus Christ,* the declared love of God. No one is ever a Christian minister who
has not come to know the reality of God's love in Christ and
has not heard within his own life and his own spirit this call
of God's concern—this call of God's reality to proclaim the
gospel of salvation without which the world has no hope.

By Jesus Christ the declared love of God and the cleansing
love of God; because this is a world that stands in need of
forgiveness and cleansing. This is an age that needs to be forgiven, to have its whole subconscious cleansed and restored
to the sanity which the Gospel alone can give when we know
that we are right with God and right with man. And by Jesus
Christ not only the declared love of God, not only the Light,
not only the cleansing of God, but also the empowering love
of God.

So very often we preach as though Jesus Christ were an
idea. And to many people, God is no more than an idea. He
is not personally real. We are concerned about the fact that
we teach our children these ideas and we preach the idea

from the pulpit, and still we have juvenile delinquency, still we have crime, still we have war, still we have divorce, still we have these things.

And our foundations are spending millions of dollars in trying to find out why when we know what is right we do not do it.

I am convinced that the reason is basically that we do not know the power of God. The early Christian church knew the power of God. You see, Jesus Christ is the point in human history where God himself broke through with his full power, because God not only became revealed, he, so to speak, made the outlet—like an electric outlet—and when one touches that place—if he really touches it—he experiences power for life and light.

An apostle by *God the Father!* There is a great danger of our getting a Jesus cult—a mere emotional association with Jesus that does not understand that the Son of God is seen in the life and reality of the Father. The Son is not only history's most high. The Son is never to be understood merely in terms of man. The Son must never be understood as *just* a man. If God is present as the summit and summary of human nature, Jesus must, of course, be understood at least in that light, or Jesus is not understood at all.

The fundamental thing about Jesus Christ, however, is that he is God himself come into history—here God has spoken, here he has walked, here he has suffered, and here he has conquered for our sake. And, therefore, we must realize that here we have, so to speak, the crucified Creator. Here in Jesus we meet the One who made the world—from nothing.

I don't know what "nothing" means, and when astronomers like Harlow Shapley of Harvard say they have come to the conclusion that the universe is made from nothing, they will find that Christian theology knew that long ago!

By creation from nothing we understand that this world is not self-sufficient and cannot be explained in terms of itself and cannot be controlled within itself, but that outside and beyond, as well as within, reality is not merely a force. Many laymen, especially, like to call God a force, but he is a person, a faithful Father, a personal Spirit. Him we can trust, him we can love, because he is truly God.

"*Who raised him up again.*" The early church preached Jesus and the Resurrection. I believe that the Christian church has lost its power because it has lost its faith in the great supernatural realities. This life is only the mere beginning of God's work. And after this life, though we cannot spell it out, there lie larger purposes and reality, so that when you bury a child—and many of you have had this experience—there you feel the touch of Presence. You are caught by a Person.

So you go home from the grave not knowing how, but with a thankful heart and a firm faith, because whatever God has taken from you that is real will remain because love cannot lose its own, *God's* own.

I hope that you will reach such an assurance because you know the reality of the power of an endless life, so that when men look up into your face all of life is taken into a new meaning and a new perspective.

I want to leave with you a personal experience that over the years has come to mean more and more to me. When I was a boy of thirteen, I left Sweden to come to this country. It was very hard because I had no money and because I had no language but Swedish. But after we as a family had read the New Testament and after we had prayed, beginning with the youngest of eight children and going through all the rest, we walked to the station. At the station there was a wonderful choir. They sang a hymn that I shall never forget.

But the memory that forms a motivating faith of my life is the memory of my mother. She wanted to say something, because she thought she might never see me again. She wanted to say something that was real and right. I could see Mother, her mouth forming words and not saying anything.

Finally the conductor blew his whistle and the train began to pull away. Just when the train moved off, Mother half ran along the platform and said, *"Nels, remember Jesus; Nels, remember Jesus."*

My word to you is very simple. In Jesus Christ we see the heart of God. Throughout your whole ministry remember Jesus raised from the dead and God the Father who raised him.

CHAPTER 11

According to Your Faith

According to your faith be it done to you. MATTHEW 9:29

All of us live by faith. To live is to make an evaluative response to the world in which we live, to the universe, to reality. No one can escape making an ultimate evaluative response, and that response is his faith. Every person is religious. Every person worships a god. The only question is, what god he worships, whom he worships. Because all of us live by faith, the question is what kind of faith, how much faith, and how real is our faith.

First of all, our faith must be right. A strong faith is not enough. Many of you may remember reading in the paper of a group of hill folk who in their simple faith took the promise of Mark 16:18 literally, that we shall drink poison as Christians and it shall not hurt us. One evening, you remember, the young minister passed a cup of poison to his young, strongly believing deacon, who lifted the cup high, thanked God for the sureness of the promises, drank, and died. When he was buried, his wife said, "My husband died from having too much faith."

Now I believe he did not die from too much faith, but from a false faith. You may remember, too, reading about a widow in Georgia who copied Abraham and murdered her only daughter because, she said, her daughter stood between her and God. She loved the daughter more than anything else and God could not be real to her. Whatever the psychological explanations are, the fact is that as far as her conscious, deliberate choice was concerned she could hardly have had more faith, but the faith was not right.

Right faith must be right outside the believer. The blind men of whom we have read came to Jesus. If they had not come to the one who could heal, they would not have been healed. Many of us fail to come to God as he has truly revealed himself, and to come to him fully. God's actual presence in human history as unconditional, universal love, the one who can always be trusted, came in Jesus Christ in fullness.

I have come to believe that the kind of God we believe in is our basic choice. God as a living God must be more than a symbol. It is all right to worship God as a symbol if by that we mean that the God we worship is ever more than anything we can understand. God must at least be as much as and more than the symbol.

We cannot stop with a symbol. We must believe that God acts and is a living God. A colleague, Langdon Gilkey, said to me that modern man's greatest offense is prayer, because if we really pray and believe that God will answer our prayer, we must presuppose a God who is real and acts in history.

A college professor consulted me, to determine whether or not he should accept an invitation to teach in a divinity school. The one question I asked him was this: "Do you, or do you not, believe that God is, and is real, and acts in history? If you do not believe that, I do not think you ought to be teaching in a divinity school."

The fundamental choice of man is whether or not he actually believes in God. Not long ago I sat in the campus grill with a student who was doing his Ph.D. thesis on two social prophets in different generations in America. He said the difference between these two men is that the one of the previous generation believed that God was metaphysically real and acted in history, whereas the other one uses exactly the same terminology very often but nothing seems to happen in history, or he does not seem to presuppose that God himself is actually with us.

Now this is a very personal and informal story, but I am

going to bare to you my heart. My wife and I were walking around the lake in Newton Centre where we live, and we were talking about the colleague who would join me there. I said I hoped he would be a man who actually believed in the full Christian message and life after death and all of these things which so often are offensive to modern man.

My wife said, "Nels, the thing to look for is whether or not the man believes in God. If a man believes in the right kind of God, then the rest will follow. It is not so much what you believe as whom you believe."

That is perfectly true. The fundamental thing is that we must come to the right source, to the right reality, and faith must be right inside, in line with God's holy will.

Now this is not an easy thing for us to accept. Very near this place, I myself went through a real choice. I had been called upon suddenly to pray with and for one of my students and his child. They had just found that the child, two years old, had leukemia. They asked me to come to their home. "We believe in spiritual healing. We believe that you are a man of prayer. Won't you come and pray for us that he be healed?"

Well, I prayed and prepared myself, and asked my wife to accompany me. We were driving along, and suddenly she said to me, "Nels, are you going to pray that the child get well?"

"I certainly am going to lift him right up to God," I said, "and if it be God's will that he be healed, I will hold him up there."

"Have you the right to do it?" my wife asked.

"Of course I have a right to do it," I said.

Then she asked, "Is it right to put false hope into the parents' hearts?"

I turned the car around, I confess to you. "If you are not going to believe," I said, "I am not going there. I am not going to have anybody along with me who does not believe. I am not going in this atmosphere."

Then she said, "It isn't because I don't believe, Nels. I

want to believe completely. If you know that the child is going to be healed, go ahead and I will support you and I will bless you. If you don't know it, I wouldn't pray for it in that way, because you should pray that they be willing to accept God's full will to live in a whole new relationship to God, to render up the child in peace, and do the best they can for the child. Then, if it be God's will, and you lift him up in this atmosphere, that will come. Don't go and teach them to kick against the pricks rather than to accept God's will."

I examined myself, and I prayed and I thought, and as usually happens, I believed my wife was right.

It is not that we have no right to pray for these things. I myself have seen wonderful things happen. The fundamental thing is that we must completely pray for God's will. The fundamental and first choice is the acceptance of God's will without any reservations. When we have done that, we can leave everything with confidence in his hands to be done in his way and to follow out our faith as never before.

The second thing we must remember is that our strength must be strong. Sören Kierkegaard said that Christianity is passion. Richard Baxter, a seventeenth-century Puritan Reformer, declared that a passionless Christianity is a contradiction in terms. Passion—true passion, Christian passion, a religious passion—comes from passivity. Very often we work up a feverish acceptance which is nothing more than our own rationalizing. When we really accept God's will, we have to learn first of all to be completely passive, to let God be God and God's will reign.

This is Pentecost. A hundred and twenty people passed fifty days praying and waiting. I wonder what would happen today to the Christian church if we really had the grace and the patience to keep waiting for God and God's will, and then were willing to do it!

You see, passivity comes from an active God who must become central to our lives if we are going to be effectively active. True passivity is necessary if we are to find God's pres-

ence. I recall an incident at Bela Vasady's home. I was visit-
ing him and his wife, having lunch, when this distinguished
professor, formerly of Prague University, said,

"My wife was a student and she looked up to me. I did all
the courting. Being a professor in Europe is different from
being a professor in the United States. She never dared to say
a word to me because I was a professor. I took all the initiative."

She smiled sweetly and replied, "But you will never know,
dear, how active I had to be to keep passive."

If we are going to have a true Christian passion, it must
come first of all from being passive. Intensity of faith, however, can never substitute for intelligence of mind. You may
have seen a man trying to lift a heavy piece of furniture up
some stairs. You come along and ask him if he doesn't know
there's an elevator just down the corridor. There are some
people who try to lift things when, if only they could let go,
they would find that there is a power lifting things from on
high, and that power can operate through their intellect
when their intellect is used by their faith. Faith never takes
the place of study, or of personal or social responsibility.
Strong faith, true faith, is always motivated by love.

We know from experience that as soon as we pray for
something and there gets mixed into it even the slightest
interest of our own, nothing happens, nor is there peace and
reality inside; but when we are allowed the grace to have no
thought but God's will, and we concentrate on some human
need, we have felt the presence and the power of God so real
that we cannot deny it. Why is it, I ask myself over and over
again, that we do not live this reality that we know so well.
History shows that it is the power of believing love that can
change the course of affairs as nothing else can.

I heard William Barclay, of Glasgow, preach, and I shall
never forget the sermon. He preached on the accusative case.
He is a Greek scholar. "Blessed are they who hunger and
thirst after righteousness." He said hungering and thirsting
after righteousness is not in the genitive but in the accusative

case. In the genitive case one drinks of the water, or in the genitive case one eats something of the plate, but in the accusative case one has to eat everything.

If we are going to find the reality and power of God, we must find it insofar as we accept the one who was wholly, unconditionally, universal love in Jesus Christ, and surrender ourselves without any qualifications in joy and peace to this love.

Christian faith, then, is real, right, and strong when Christ as God's Word becomes central to us as men—universal, unconditional, and our final authority. God is the personal spirit who is the infinite holy Love, and Christ is the spirit who disclosed this love and in whom it is self-attested.

The Holy Spirit today is waiting for a new Pentecost. Perhaps the deepest thing that I have to say or leave with you is that I believe the Holy Spirit to be God actually available to each person now according to his own need and in his own way; that God is not dead, but that God is available for every one under every circumstance. I believe that God is here to give us a strong and right faith through the Holy Spirit, to give us an inclusive community and open communications in all areas of life.

More and more we hear statements such as that of the English scientist, C. P. Snow, before a gathering of American scientists to the effect that either we go on letting the small nations get the bomb, in which case destruction sooner or later becomes inevitable, or we find courage and wisdom to enter a new age of international co-operation and control. We must find grace negatively to disarm and positively to build up a constructive world community based on trust and common concern.

I have often thought about this. Are we heading for a final catastrophe, or are we heading for a new age? My own conviction is that we are free and either can happen. My real hope is that as God holds the nations in his hands, as well as our personal lives, he can find enough faith for his purpose to be accomplished. God has shifted the gears of history.

God has put before us a blessing and a curse, and my own deepest faith is that if we will be true to what has been disclosed to us in Jesus Christ and trust him, we can see the power to give us the new age that is signified by this day— the coming of the Spirit on Pentecost.

CHAPTER 12

A Charge to Your City

. . . from his presence earth and sky fled away, and no place was found for them. REVELATION 20:11

Before God's presence the evils of the world must fly away, and no place be found for them. At certain times in human history God draws peculiarly ne r, to demand either a change or destruction. Our day is such a time. It may not be the end of the world, but then it must be the end of an era.

Strategically, your city is at the center of American life. American life is now central to world history. Who can foretell your city's place and power in American thought and life? I pray for its fullest use in Christian and world leadership. In this spirit I give this charge to your city:

I

I charge your city to accept and to live a universal religion. True religions are born, not manufactured. They cannot be produced; they grow. A man-made religion is a house made of straw. It cannot stand the strain of our days. And yet we must prepare for the universal religion that shall match the critical and creative need of this hour. I charge your city so to prepare.

The universal religion must be as high as the heart of God. No lesser faith will do. Faith shapes life and determines man's destiny. Man's temptation is to find truth by the scaling down of his hope. He seeks it in minimum hypothesis whereas he can find it only in maximum faith. He searches for security in critical thinking rather than in creative believing. Therefore he fails, and keeps failing. Man is made to scale the heights, not to scale down his aspirations. Truth is for the taking. The heart of God is breaking with longing for men of faith.

Compromise is reduction. We need re-creation. "Co-operation without compromise" is not enough. No religion in its present formulation is sufficiently ample for the world's new-felt need. Even the Christian faith, at least as traditionally formulated, is far overrated.

The heart of God is too high for ingroup devotion. The fences between religions, however high, are more horizontal than vertical. As we go up, we go over them. God's heart is for all; man's faith is too small. The higher we reach, the smaller our difference. Both Gentile and Jew, as St. Paul knew, worship one God. Both Christian and pagan have one God in common. None knows him too well and all serve him the worse.

When we start believing, we start receiving. All things are shaking. God only stands firm. The higher we venture in the quality of faith, the fuller the finding that binds us together. Religion can be sufficiently broad only when it dares to aspire in faith as high as the heart of God.

A universal religion is not only as high as the heart of God, but also as wide as human need. God's love covers all. Have ye not known that the Lord never fails and that by reason of his strength not one is outside God's concern? He not only numbers, but names all. God's love is as particular as each person and as parochial as each parish.

What are religions to him but man-made theologies and practices penetrated by man's fears and mixed with his finitude? As each flower and tree has a right to the sun, so each person and people has a right to his God. God's love is as indiscriminate as the sun, calling all, drawing all, strengthening all who respond to its rays. That religion alone is true that dares to affirm all men's right of way to the sun and exerts itself to remove whatever keeps the sun away.

If the Christian way is universal, it is so only because it refuses to set limits to the love of God. Nothing human is alien to God, except our refusal of his love, and nothing human can be alien to those who call on his name. Sin there is; ignorance there is; failure there is—yes, yes, and yes again.

But we worship not what tears us apart but what holds us together. If God made peoples and races, why not religions? Does he who glorified creation with diversity mind difference in faith and worship? If God is love, the God of the Christ-heart, the only orthodoxy is the spirit of universal love. God's standard is inclusive concern within integrity of faith.

Utopian and contrary to the ways of God are all attempts to unify the world within one organization, even though it style itself the universal church. The true universal religion is the common worship through all religions of the One who is high and lifted up and whose only begotten Son is the Son of Man, the Son we all should become in order to be our real selves. If we call ourselves Christians, it can be only because in Jesus, in an exceptional historic way, that Son was born. Can accepting Christ mean less than acknowledging God's potential presence in all men? Does it not mean that religion must be lifted as high as the heart of God and stretched as wide as human need?

A universal religion must be not only as high as the heart of God and as wide as human need, but also as deep as human depravity. All too often have religions that aim at height and width refused to see the low. But sin is a fact, an awful fact, a most stubborn fact. Not to diagnose the killing cancer is to kill the patient with kindness. Such kindness is blind, but not love. Love faces the facts and finds faith to change them.

Depravity is about to destroy us. Sin leads to death and today's sin to the death of mankind. Repent we must or reap we shall the wages of sin. No charge to your city is more than soft words that dare not announce our decision: repent or die. God wants to forgive sin, to free us from fear, to restore us to sanity, by lifting us to love, and to release our creative selves for fulfilling community.

A universal religion is born, not made; it grows and can-not be manufactured. But the unity of the universal religion will come through the richness of the many religions, as we let ourselves be lifted by faith as high as the heart of God, expanded in our concern as wide as human need, and humbled as deep as human sin. No other religion will do; such a faith will never fail. I charge your city to accept and to live a universal religion.

II

I also charge your city to produce and practice a centered education. Today is the day of education, higher and lower. We worry because we lag behind Russia in this respect. Russia has a centered education. It is oriented within Marx-ist ideology. It knows where it is going and what it is about. Our concern is misplaced. Our anxiety should spring out of our lack of centeredness whereby we are failing the world in its critical need for educated leadership. I charge your city, therefore, to produce and to practice a centered education equal to today's need.

A centered education gives main directedness with con-crete devotion. Our centeredness is in democracy under God. Democracy under God is for all the people, by all the people, without limit of loyalty. Such democracy encourages freedom of search, freedom of finding, freedom of telling, and free-dom of doing the truth.

A centered education makes basic the free, co-operative method of establishing and disseminating the truth. All creeds that divide and all tests that oppress the human spirit are alien to an education centered in democracy under God. The richness of reality cannot be reduced to the relativity of religious sects, to the price of social position, or to the fear of power-driven politicians. Democracy under God cen-ters in community of education. It specializes in the public school. It fosters general learning through all states of life.

That society decays which mushrooms private schools for

the pleasure of status seekers. That society becomes divided against itself that substitutes parochial education for the common training of its young in the rich plurality of its confessions.

That society is already paralyzed by fear that fetters the freedom of faith within either unnecessary or inane loyalty oaths. For certain reasons there may be legitimate need for private schools; some sects, of course, may have to protect their vulnerable faith behind parochial walls; and some political systems may have to muzzle their teachers to protect themselves against true and full democracy.

But democracy under God knows no such bounds; through its public schools it fosters the free and co-operative society, cultivating the positive values of our common humanity; and through its concrete devotion it spurns all external tests of loyalty.

A centered education enhances local loyalty. It cannot serve the state at the expense of the family or the church. Democracy under God knows the irreplaceable need for home and religion. Co-operation in education never means reduction in the concrete vividness of faith. But it knows that all truths essential for education can be taught freely together from all homes of body, mind, and spirit.

Many parents in communities where public education lags far behind private, have sacrificed the more intimate affections of class or church, and even what may at short range seem the advantage of the child, by sending their child to public school for the sake of the public education for democracy where all can learn to know each other, rich and poor, cultured and common, Catholic and Protestant, Jew or any other faith, believing that American leadership in this critical hour of world history hangs on its education being centered in democracy under God. I therefore charge your city to produce and practice such an education.

A centered education, moreover, gives personal integrity with committed concern. There is an educational heresy in the air to the effect that freedom in education means freedom from religion. Absolutes are supposed to make for intolerance. What preposterous nonsense! Religion is our basic evaluation of life. No civilization can be without that.

Education without religion is adrift. The opposite of the absolute is relativism. The logic of relativism is that education is without final standards. The fault is not in religion or in absolutes, but in inferior religions and in divisive or oppressive absolutes. Personal integrity and committed concern go together.

Freedom is found within the absolute truth of God the good for all, whose service is perfect freedom, and whose worship is the final faith. God never forces faith. Humbly he encourages our free search for him, until we find that the way of self is most truly the way of society, while the way of society is most fully the way of God's concern for the common good.

A centered education also gives loyalty to our historic heritage along with creative community. Real education is never rootless liberalism; it is never abstract universalism. No one is educated who does not cherish his particular past. The tutored spirit is never ungrateful. Lack of loyalty to our own heritage is a failure of learning as well as of spirit; it is to live in the superficial pride of our own achievement which we owe mostly to those who made it possible for us. The appropriation of the past is the power for creative community.

History is like a river flowing forward. Only those who know how to ride its surging center can advance creatively to new destinies. To interpret natural science as the surging center, the temptation of our time, is to forfeit the fullness of the long rise of human history where the meaning of science has always been fullness of knowledge in all its branches in the service of man.

We Americans have a heritage of democracy under God, rich and powerful beyond imagination, waiting to pay its rich interest to all who appreciate the deposit. Within that democracy there are many divisions in the main stream that flow in the same direction, that enrich the scenery and vary the journey.

Central directedness can provide not only concrete devotion in the present but the enriching heritage of our past. Personal integrity is fulfilled by becoming committed within such concerns. A centered education spurns only drifting and dogmatism, that is to say, lack of central directedness or making private or parochial interest central to the education task, and fettering education within externally enforced loyalty to political systems, whether based on property or on the proletariat.

I charge your city, in this day of decision, to produce and practice a centered education, a free and full democratic education under God.

III

I charge your city to establish and to cultivate an open society. The critical question, I take it, between communism and any idea of the Christian society, is our espousal of an open society. We sin against our ideal, but, that we have it as an ideal, is significant. The fundamental decision is not economic, however important that may be, but concerns the nature of the kind of community we cherish. I charge your city to establish and to cultivate an open society.

An open society rises above class, without colorless commonness. Those of us who came from Europe dread a class-ridden society. We are fast getting there. We are increasingly class conscious. When Vance Packard, the popular writer on the current American scene, charges that nearly all Americans are insecure as to their social standing, inadequate as to their attainment, and are in fact status seekers, he is right. We are not settled, but on the move. We conform to patterns for belonging prescribed for us by society. I think a class-chasing society is worse than a class-ridden society. In a class-ridden society there is at least a certain security of belonging. I charge your city to reverse this trend to decay by producing a social surge for creative openness.

Such openness is never a matter of leveling down or of pushing up. It is rather the free, realistic acceptance of people as people, both for what they are and for what they are worth. When people are accepted for what they are there is freedom to move from stratum to stratum without artificial barriers either of attitude or of standards, and wherever they are, they are accepted for themselves. Such movement in the open society depends on worth of character and on achievement.

Both the hankering for a classless society and the hungering for the freezing of society where it is are bad. All attempts to make people equal, except in opportunity, sin against God who created us unequal. Even the attempt to make ministers' salaries equal, as in British Methodism, I believe to be a revolt against the Creator.

Nothing in nature or man is equal. We should accept this elementary fact and make the most of it. An open society provides the fullest opportunity for each and all to make the most of life. Each should accept himself and should be accepted by society for what he is and has achieved. That people differ in talents and gifts, in power and money, should be the natural assumption based on God's creation and man's varying use of God's endowment. There should be common respect, and neither pride nor envy.

The reality of community should make all, freely or under necessity, contribute to a common reservoir of resources whatever makes for the fullest opportunity for all. Thus the more gifted in talent and achievement would not be deprived of whatever fuller resources could enrich their lives, make them creative, and find maximum fulfillment of life; while the less talented or less industrious would still receive whatever opportunities were needed for them to contribute to society and to find their maximum of meaningful existence.

An open society is thus realistic and concerned, just and creative, secure and flexible. An open society is a mature society in spirit and in the handling of social status and economic reward. Common opportunity is wedded to a common acceptance of people for what they are and for what they accomplish.

An open society also rises above race, without forced acceptance. When the Supreme Court had given its famous final verdict on this question, I preached at Fisk, a Negro university. I expected jubilation. Instead there was relief, mixed with the firm insistence that opportunity without acceptance is empty. Segregation can be broken on buses without being broken in spirit. Ralph Bunche may gain membership in a famous tennis club, and still be an outsider. Restriction may be banned in housing, and enforced, without Negroes becoming a part of our neighborhoods.

To rise above race without forced acceptance does not mean any lessening of full opportunities for all races in every dimension of public life: political, social, and economic. On the contrary, it means full integration based on the free acceptance of all in public and private life, because of a mature relation motivated by high religion and effected by wise education. Acceptance will be denied or forced until the springs of our lives are cleansed by universal religion and made natural, and ready, through a centered education.

Your city is increasingly involved in the problem of race. The world as well as the country is weighed down by the grief of racial irrationality and immaturity. I charge your city, in the name of God and of our common welfare, to produce and cultivate an open society which rises above race, without forced acceptance.

An open society also rises above nation, without loss of patriotism. Nationalism can destroy us, but so can internationalism and supernationalism. They can become empty substitutes for loyalty to the land as the largest concrete embodiment of social order. Just as a housewife may snatch at "causes" to take the place of happiness at home, so people can espouse internationalism as a way of atoning for lack of national devotion and attention to duty. We shall get together as a family of nations within one law and order only when whatever common rule is now a necessity becomes the fulfillment of national loyalty. World law and world rule are no longer optional; they are necessary for survival, but they cannot take the place of patriotism.

What we need now is more than intellectual stretching to keep up with the world-wide organization of human community; we need emotional growth into the maturity of a new age that has suddenly been forced upon us. Such intellectual expansion and emotional growth can come now, quickly enough to help us, only from a spiritual reconstruction in new dimensions motivating a reoriented education. An open society depends upon a centered education and a centered education needs the strength of universal religion.

Before God, in that awful day, "earth and sky fled away, and no place was found for them." Today the day of the Lord may be nearer than we think. There is surely no place for the world as we have known it. We have to adjust to God's new day or die.

My hope and prayer, yes, and my faith, is that we shall enter the new age with new vistas and new powers for human community. For it we need a new dimension, a universal religion, a centered education, and an open society, not as escapist abstractions, not as utopian dreams, but as the concrete fulfillment of our best loyalties and leadership. Your city (insofar as important to what may be the world's most dangerous nation) is increasingly important to the world's destiny. May America never become so pathological by frustrated fright that it dare countenance a war of annihilation. Many there are who are more afraid of Russia than of God, who prefer death in war to the loss of the cold-war race.

Our only ultimate loyalty must be to God in his inclusive concern for all men. I charge your city to find and to cultivate such universal concern anchored in reality.

God grant to your city sanity of faith and creativity of hope, until enough love of mankind leavens our national life to let us lead, or at least go along with, a haggard world into an era of constructive civilization. I charge your city to live and so to lead!

CHAPTER 13

Expanding Horizons

In the year that King Uzziah died I saw the Lord sitting upon a throne, high and lifted up. ISAIAH 6:1

This is the day of decision. Every day is a day of decision for each and for all, but this day we may be deciding concerning life or death for human history. The day when Uzziah died in Israel of long ago is now upon us. Our day calls for a faith with radically expanding horizons. I have seldom prayed more earnestly and for a more significant event than for the summit meeting, which could turn out to have been humanity's last chance for survival. But the things which belonged to our peace were then shut from our eyes, and we preferred fear and private profit to order and universal plenty.

Some of us, to see the other side, had been gladdened by the unbelievably clear-seeing and unanimous report of the six-hundred-member Commission on World Order at Cleveland in 1959, representing the National Council of Churches, calling for a radical doing to death of the cold war, for the admission of Soviet China into the United Nations, and for other equally compelling actions.

Protestantism stood officially, as in the Cleveland Conference on World Order, for the Camp David spirit, but the industrial-military alliance of greed and power, against which President Eisenhower warned in his farewell address to the nation, countered with a disastrous war alert and a notorious spy flight. Protestantism faced the Pentagon and seemingly lost.

Thus do some of us foolish human beings put our trust

in princes and assemblies, but our Uzziahs, however great, die and are gone. No new Pentecost of unanimous believers in church decisions or with regard to political events will save us now. Nor will some purely political decision, even on a world-wide scale, insure our salvation. Only the God high and lifted up whom Isaiah, in his despair and bewilderment, beheld in the temple, can save.

I

Kings die! Do you remember how Fénelon opened his funeral sermon at the death of Louis XIV? "God alone is great." Our greatest need today, have no doubt about it, is new-found faith in God, the living God, the God who acts in judgment or deliverance. If we will only know the day of our peace! The prophets of the Old Testament never counted the armies of Cyrus, but trusted the mighty arm of the Lord revealed. The apostolic church cried no help from people, but from the living God for whom they died and with whom in dying they won their witness. The Reformers may have had help of princes, but their real power was declared in their defiant shout, "Here I stand, I can do no other; so help me God." Human history is no pretty picture. The best side to its face is the persistent daring of men and women of great faith. Such faith moved the masses, but proved too hard for them. Human tragedy continues.

Uzziah is dead. Our chance now is for us to see God high and lifted up. Only horizons expanding with the fuller view of God now count. Our hope now is for a high-enough faith, and a general-enough faith, to change the direction of human history. Norman Cousins is right: destruction or a new level of living. There is no other choice.

The new-found faith in God can be no narrow faith. Can we forget our scientific knowledge? Can we bypass our critical sense of history? Can we ignore the challenge of linguistic analysis? Can we get around the confrontation with other religions? Can we cover up our own self-indulgent and defiled living that paralyzes faith? There is no retreat now into the past.

For hope, there is now only the choice of the greater God, the incommensurate God, who holds in his hands life or death. No idol and no human prejudice, only the determiner of destiny, the God high and lifted up will do. We have to accept faith in the supremacy of God whose conditions for life are righteousness and universal concern beyond any present attainment.

I suggest that God is hard to find. We cry with Job, "Oh, that I knew where I might find him" (23:3). There is no going back to Christ away from modern knowledge. Infantilism in religion cannot save us now. Our comfort in this day of decision must be courage, not man-blown but God-inspired, as we face the ever-widening horizons of the modern world view.

Aghast we run back to Christ and find him gone, for he is not in the past. Status-quo Christianity is thoroughly discredited. Nor can we make faith out of modern knowledge. It squeezes us to death or stretches us to nothingness. Christ is in the modern knowledge, and for a new faith, only when we keep looking at him and at the modern knowledge at the same time.

We need now both the intimacy of the biblical Christ and the ultimacy of the God of the sidereal spaces. The immeasurable immensities test our faith in the concrete Christ. The holy life of Love in Jesus Christ our Lord is the infinitesimal center of the endless immensities who alone lights up the face of the faithful God who is both top and bottom of every bottomless abyss of man's ignorance and despair. Knowledge without meaning offers futility; meaning without an organizing center provides confusion; Jesus Christ as God's universal love gives central meaning both to life and death, both to work and destiny.

II

And his presence filled the temple. The God high and
lifted up was also right there! Too often the God who is high
and lifted up is clear away from man's problems. Man flees
from his troubles into some fancied realm of divine transcendence. The great God beyond man's thinking and hold-
ing who alone is Lord is love's actual presence in the midst
of man's problems. His presence fills the temple.

And not only the holy of holies. We fence God off into
sacred and most sacred, and into secular and more secular
still. The true God fills the whole temple. In the earthly
temple only the high priest could enter the holy of holies
once a year. In God's true temple that Isaiah saw, God was
everywhere and accessible to all. There was no division between priest and people, Jew and Gentile, man and woman,
free and slave. His presence filled the temple. God is for all,
all the time. Have we caught that vision yet?

Have we matured enough yet to recover the inner unity
of faith with all faiths? Is our religion as wide as and wider
than all religions? Faith is man's response. Religions are man-
made. God is greater than all faiths and wider than all religions. Let faiths die. Let religions perish. God remains. He
whose glory we have seen in the face of Jesus Christ has not
left himself without a witness anywhere.

Do we recognize that witness? Do we accept the witnesses?
Can religion become a bridge beyond our destructive divisiveness carrying us to some common mainland of integrity
and love? Can religion reveal the wideness of God's mercy
who will destroy our deathly narrowness? Can Christianity
prove its true nature by losing its institutional self-concern?
Can its faith prove its own intrinsic worth by its openness
to truth beyond the safe limits of suffocating fences?

God will carry on what is eternally true, right, and needed
in our faith when we use it in concern for the faith beyond
faiths that will include and can save us all. If truth be truth

and love be truth, need we fear adventure in faith large enough to cover the face of the earth? Do we believe in the fenced-off God behind some body of holies in our own temple, guarded by our own high priests of dogma, or can we too see the presence of God filling the whole temple of mankind?

When God's presence fills the whole temple, social and political issues are not roped off within some private pews. Péguy said that religion begins in mysticism and ends in politics. God reaches into politics too. If we will let him, he will help us. If we won't let him, he will judge us. Our way is to fence off; his way is to fill the whole temple with his glory. Today we need a new deal in world politics.

Our horizons must expand unimaginably. The day of the sovereignty of nations is dead. Only the world community can live. Nations are now branches not the trunk of human history. Brinkmanship is bunk. Militarism is madness. It is the realism of nothing but the dead burying their dead. Slogans can't save us, but they can blind us to the fact of our situation. We shout freedom and mean privilege. We shout faith and mean ingroup psychology. We shall not be saved unless we repent and reform.

I see two possible escapes from world catastrophe in atomic annihilation. One is that communism will sweep the world with its stern puritanism. Then, of course, there will be no world war of total destruction. Before its austere commitment our cancan decadence, our liquored moral blur, our fashion-tied economy, our surplus-rotting, price-pegged American way of life, rooted and grounded in production for war, smeared with cosmetic superficiality over the scab of self-indulgence, may cave in at the hate-filled shrieks and the life-indifferent mobs of our desperate youth whose very chance to live we deny.

The ax of God's inexorable judgment is already laid to the root of our own tree. The decline of the West has become its destruction. Asia and Africa will rise up in judgment and the poison of our own sustained and abandoned sinning will paralyze us beyond any effective defense. There is hope for the world in our collapse, if that prevents world destruction, putting upon all dedicated Christians the fearsome task of living and dying for freedom and faith within a strange home of head and heart. God can still call his Cyrus out of Russia or China to save the world. We may have to lose our lives in our endeavor to Christianize communism from within.

Or as a nation we can repent and reform. We can accept the self-discipline that is true freedom. We can negotiate with sincerity and good will and not with spyflights and war alerts. We can use and not prostitute the United Nations from Korea to the Congo. We can share our means of production more than our products; our initiative and our income with half our desperate world. We can disarm and plan our economy for peace. No one who is realistically aware of what is going on in the world can deny the prophetic realism of these utterances. God is not mocked, nor does he sleep.

We can discipline our means of communication into carriers of news and education instead of hate and propaganda. We must become willing to listen to objective truth instead of slanting all news to support our side.

We can reform our education into creative faith and controlled inquiry instead of cynical skepticism and naturalistic reductionism.

We can firm our flabby moral muscles into creative rectitude. We can dethrone the triumvirate of profit, liquor, and sex as the ruling attractions of life and, instead of them, accept the reign of God, high and lifted up, whose presence fills the whole temple of life with moral satisfaction, social fulfillment, and public welfare. The latest figure I have seen on crime is murder, attempted murder and rape in the United States every fourth minute; a car stolen every other minute. But the figures are expected to go far even beyond that! Where are we going? When indecision leads to disaster, to drift is to die.

Our second choice, which should be our first concern, is our own repentance and the coming of a new reformation. "Why will ye die?" cries the prophet of old. Death will, of course, come to us all and very likely unexpectedly. But why not live all our lives here on earth by a turning to the fount of life? No peace goes deeper than righteousness and no freedom is fuller than freedom in the right. He who really loves life craves the willing and determined turning of our feet into the paths of peace.

Our need now is increasingly a new social structure and open social attitudes. The recent volume by Walter Lord, *The Good Years,* dealing with the beginning of this century in the United States, portrays a world where wealth and social standing were commonly accepted at the expense of brutal exploitation of child labor and seemingly endless working hours for all who toiled. We need a new world beyond race, beyond money, beyond name, beyond position, based on intellectual alertness and social contribution. We need a worldwide revolution which glories in inner character and public service. We need God's new age for the common good.

I thank God for living now. The old order is dying. It is both decaying and drying up. It is disintegrating from within and being destroyed from without. This is the day of danger. This is the day of opportunity. This is the day of danger. Let our faith keep pace with our expanding horizons or else collapse the shell of Christian confession. Why mock the living God by our masks of piety?

In the day when the old order must be dead and faith must find new horizons, what shall we say of religious divisiveness, what shall we say of Christian divisiveness, what shall we say of Protestant divisiveness even within the United Church of Christ? In the day when God's people must save the world by standing together, are there not some in our midst who stand apart even from the most democratic church conceivable that incarnates full freedom with effective fellowship within a unanimously accepted statement of faith and a unanimously accepted constitution?

Let us not judge. Let us not exorcise. Let us not add grief to misunderstanding, smallness of vision, and misdirected loyalty. Let us, rather, pray and love and persevere, until the greatness of God's grace and the desperateness of the world's need fill all who hesitate with an unbearable longing to be done with the old load of critical over-againstness and to be lost within the warm community of creative openness.

Let the past die and within it let us bury all unworthy words and feelings. Let larger horizons call forth the fuller faith and the firmer fellowship.

III

In the temple God spoke to one. He addressed Isaiah.

God wants you! Do you see the vision of God high and lifted up, whose presence fills the whole temple of mankind? Then answer: Woe is me, for I am undone. I am undone. I am unclean and my people is unclean. If you will commit your life to his command the angel will blister your lips with a coal from the altar of reality. You will be burned, for thus alone can you be healed and sent. There is no easy way out. Your wounds must be cauterized. You must be forgiven and remade. God needs you to be a messenger to cover your face with two wings of humility, to cover your feet with two wings of reverence, and fly with the other two to tell of God's way of deliverance where all human help fails. The local idols of class and creed topple. Only the true God equal to man's universal needs can save the world for a new day.

We have been sold down the river by the false prophets of our time. They have baptized secular social science with its opportunistic power politics, omnipotent to save, into the holy name of Christian realism. They have deified history and called it unchangeable except for the teetering on the constant brink of a justice, unattained and mocking. This is human realism, arrogating to itself the name of divinity.

History, to be sure, is man's constant defeat apart from God. History exhibits man's freedom to revolt from God and to face the results of insecurity, disintegration, and destruction. But history is also changed for the better by its great saints and seers who are open to the expanding horizons of human need and God's help. Such power to change history, and such alone, is Christian realism. Usually these prophets and saints are killed, as were Socrates, Jesus, and Gandhi, but their work goes on. Others are free to heed their lives and to join them. If enough did so, history would be radically changed. This fact is our only chance now. History is flexible to faith. In itself it is neither good nor bad. It is open and we should be expectant. Are you ready to be touched by God's fear-devouring fire and to be sent as a messenger of true hope?

Can such a change take place? May I venture a human guess. History at bottom is one as is nature. Well has Teilhard de Chardin written, as a scientist in *The Phenomenon of Man*:

"Immensity represents the action common to all atoms. The volume of each of them is the volume of the universe. The atom is no longer the microscopic, closed world we may have imagined to ourselves. It is the infinitesimal centre of the world itself."

True enough. A great life reaches all lives. The Christ when he is lifted up draws all men. The problem is not time and space of communication, but the quality of the reality that enters any life. All life at bottom is one in God and no life fails of its proper influence, however short or physically circumscribed. A few lives open to the healing love of reality can change a community; deeper or more lives can change the region; enough lives of spiritual power and lives of genuine spiritual quality can change world history. Don't blame the world for the destruction that engulfs you. Accept yourself as an agent of God's salvation here and now.

You must be changed from within. Developed from within. Illumed and empowered from within. Receive the vision of God within you. You need to be radically changed by God's forgiveness and redoing. You need a total retooling for your new task of helping to save human history.

Consider one example of power in history: Once Cornell sent out a John R. Mott. It is reported that one of America's

greatest theologians became a new man, became converted
and committed, by observing the look on the face of John R.
Mott as he went to work each day. John R. Mott believed
that the world could be evangelized in one generation. Did
anything help more to release missionary forces than his life
of faith and work? If the full work remained undone it was
because he was not joined by enough and by deep-enough
believers. Many idealists joined him and discredited his
cause. Many optimists joined him and clouded his achievement. Idealism and optimism are human feelings and must
fail. Without the vision of God the people perish. Without
being sent they have no message. Without being forgiven
they have no power. Those who respond "Here am I, send
me" must have seen the Lord high enough to fill the whole
temple of mankind. They must have no God less lifted up
than the full welfare of all men, and their lips must be burnt
and singed clean with coals from God's holy altar of truth
and concern.

The task is incredibly hard and seems hopeless. Who will
go? Whom can we send? Who can gaze at God's expanding
horizons? Broad is the way to destruction and most walk in
it. Narrow is the way to life and few find it. The life they
find they cannot lose, although they often lose what seems
the only life to the children of destruction. Will you in this
hour of critical need be the one to open your life to the
divine presence that cannot stop with you, if he fills you, but
will fill the whole temple?

Will you be a messenger of world renewal, within faith in
the large God and his universal presence? History's only
final proof of God will be within you and from your life.
Eternity rests with God. You can live a normal self-anxious
life of ordinary success and sorrow or you can make your life
significant for God and others by a total abandoning of your
will to God's concern for the common good. This is your day
of decision.

King Uzziah is dead. The boundaries of his era have been
smashed. Long live the new era of common man and the

general good. Long live God's new age of faith, of integrity, and of concern. Long live righteousness and holiness. Long live world law and world rule. Long live the united and uniting Church of Christ.

We may go to exile and destruction, as did Israel of long ago. Or with Judah we may fall, only to have a remnant survive. Or we may save the world for civilization within a new repentance and a new level of living. Life, in any case, is not first of all up to the world. It is not first of all up to the church.

Life is up to you. For your life this day you must decide. God needs your decision. Will you cling to the old order? Will you panic in no order? Or will you be sent as a messenger of God's new order? This is your day of deciding for life or death. You cannot control world history and therefore you cannot decide for or against external victory. But you can decide for faith or for failure of faith. You can decide for or against God. God give you grace to decide aright.

CHAPTER 14

The City of Confusion

The city of confusion is broken down. . . . ISAIAH 24:10

Jerusalem lay situated between Assyria and Egypt, two great military powers. For personal gain and power some of the city's inhabitants would run for help to Assyria and others to Egypt. The prophet, according to one interpretation of this passage, had warned them that sooner or later they would thus embroil Jerusalem in a war between these powers. The city basically had to be a city either of order or of confusion, a city of harmony or of contrary purposes, a city of peace or a city of strife. The people had chosen to remain a city of confusion. The doom had now come.

Today it would be easy to think of the city of confusion in terms of our national or international situation. Prophetic sermons need to be preached on this passage. Observe how devastatingly this almost unparalleled chapter describes our present situation. Instead, I want to speak about a city which we all know most intimately, the stronghold of self. For you and I are either cities of peace or cities of confusion.

I

A person may be a city of confusion for many reasons. Let me mention three of them before suggesting how the Gospel applies to such cities.

A person may be a city of confusion because of something that happened to him of which he is not now aware. We tend to think of life too much in neatly reasonable or moral terms. The hardest part of our lives to deal with, however, is the part which we cannot ourselves see or know. Some things about which we feel guilty we suppress; they cause conscious conflict. Other things we repress below our power to recall; those cause us the worst confusion. George W. Groddeck, a German psychiatrist, says that it is truer that our lives live us than that we live our lives. Besides our repressions there are also deep drives stemming from early loyalties or prejudices which impel us so strongly that mere thinking or conscious deciding seems to do little or no good. We remain cities of confusion.

A great philosopher tells somewhere how he once lunched with a very liberal Jew who took pride in being liberated from all religious inhibitions. This Jew had been brought up in Malta within a most rigidly orthodox faith. Unwittingly, he had for some time been enjoying spareribs on the menu, not knowing that they were pork. When for this lunch he ordered some, the philosopher commented upon his liberal spirit. Immediately he grew pale and ill!

A leading seminary professor, brought up in South Carolina, told me how he felt as a graduate student in a Northern university when a Negro first sat down next to him at table. In his conscious mind he had already succeeded in believing that such eating together was right. When the Negro actually came toward his seat, however, the reciting of all the Bible verses he could think of about our being of one blood and one in Christ did not save him from a shaking physical reaction. Our past is there, stronger than we imagine, causing confusion.

A person may be a city of confusion because of the nature of his environment. A mother of three lovely children came with her husband from Sweden to the United States to give her family a better economic chance. After a time she became a violent mental case and had to be sent to an institution. There she stayed for years. The psychiatrist finally concluded that she was just enough unbalanced not to be able to stand a strange environment. Upon being returned to her native land, she carried on a normal life.

In a Pullman car one night a denominational official told me how his son, who was being trained as a commando in World War II, refused to stay at home more than a few minutes of his first furlough, but packed up and went back to camp. He could not stand the contrast between his Christian home life and his commando practice. One environment or the other, he insisted, but to take part in both would mean going mad.

A person may be a city of confusion because of conflict between his actual self and the self he wants to be. Some of us may have promised God never again to become angry. During the next temptation we behaved well for a while, silently enduring abuse in business, school, or at home. But all of a sudden, we began to feel warmth spreading up from below, our head felt a bit lighter, and before we knew what was happening our tongue lashed out. What regrets followed!

Or we may have sworn never to hurt anyone, least of all by the passing on of some tidbit about him which we have heard. All may have gone well, until, all at once, our guard seems to be down and we let our tongue wag irresponsibly. What self-incriminations! Both those who confess the Christian faith and those who do not may have felt all too intimately the depth and stubbornness of sin. Cities of confusion we are, as long as we try to remain independent. The prophet knew that Jerusalem had to serve either God or evil foreign powers.

Fortunately, no city of confusion can remain so forever. Every city of confusion is besieged with evil too strong to be resisted permanently. Someday and in some way every city that tries to remain self-sufficient must fall. When a besieged city resists the enemy, it cuts itself off from supplies. How many people think that they can resist evil merely by shutting it out! All the while, however, their inner resources are being used up, and they begin to starve morally and spiritually. How sad it is to see countless people with no joy, no inner peace, no triumphal marches. Moralism is a weary

watch and cannot last forever. Self-righteousness is the grad-
ual starving of self. Yet how many depend upon it, both in
and out of our churches! However self-strong any city may
feel, it is yet confusion within and its supplies cannot last
forever.

Or a besieged city can yield to the enemy. It can give up
the moral and spiritual fight altogether, thus expecting to
ease the conflict. Occupied territory, however, is never free
from confusion. It is caught in constant strife. When sin
conquers, it breaks down peace increasingly. After all, the
evil world is full of conflicting forces which keep claiming
the conquered. To follow the path of least resistance is to
court the most trouble.

II

Fortunately, however, the city of confusion can raise the
seige by calling in a power it has falsely dreaded, which is
strong enough to overcome any and every enemy. By being
thus conquered the city can be set free. The oppressed heart
can surrender to God. The city of confusion can become a
city of peace. Such surrender is not to lose but to find freedom, for peace consists of the fullness of satisfactory relationship, freely chosen, which can be had only in God and through
his power. God is love, and to love is to set free. Surrender
to God is like surrender to a surgeon who can remove the
evil condition and thus free the body.

What happens, however, to the city of confusion with
regard to its guilt or conflicting drives from the past? God is
just to forgive our sins. There is nothing in the past which
he does not know insofar as it persists in the present to haunt
us within our subconscious life. And God is forever completely for us. That is the Gospel. We keep him from us by
our fears and our sins. Whatever is not of faith, says the
Bible, is sin. When we trust his forgiving love, however, he
frees us from our fears and forgives our sins. Perfect love
both casts out fear and forgives sins. God can use the psy-

chiatrist as well as the minister, but in the long last only God can cure the human spirit. Confidence in a psychotherapist is only a temporary substitute for trust in God. Deep and long may be the healing, but in God's time and way, he can turn every city of confusion into a city of order.

You see, all the past there is, is *now,* in the present. The past *was,* but *is* no more. The year 1800 was but is no more. All there *is* of 1800 is with us *now.* But since all the past of human history and of your life and mine is in the present and is part of us, any change in the present means also organically a change in all the past. The meaning of this change may have to be worked out over a long time, but such change of the past is real. When God forgives, he also helps us to restore the past, to remake it, to make it a clean, strong force for future good.

A city of confusion resulting from the threat of a strange or of an evil environment can also call in the supreme Power to raise its siege. God is immeasurably greater than all evils. Whoever finds genuine security in him finds inner peace to overcome any outer circumstance. Neither life nor death nor any other creature shall be able to separate us from the love of God in Christ Jesus, the Bible promises, and therefore we are more than conquerors over all evil. The almost unbelievable secret of Christian experience is that it can glory in afflictions and find joy even in a cross set before it. He who is stayed on God shall not be moved. His house is built on rock and his heart is fixed in heaven.

When the first atomic bomb fell, our family lived in Greater Boston. My wife and I decided to tell our children about it, in order that they might be prepared to hear the news from others. After we had had our usual morning devotions—our hymn, our Bible reading, and prayers on the part of all the members of the family—I told the children that a new kind of explosive had been invented by which all of Boston might someday be blown up. Frederick, twelve years old, immediately replied, "But, Daddy, it can't hurt us." I thought he had been reading *Popular Mechanics* or some such periodical and asked, "What do you mean, Frederick?" He looked at me with his serious eyes and said, "Daddy, don't you know that nothing can ever hurt a Christian?" He did not mean that God would prevent the bomb from falling. He had learned rather that whether we live or die we live or die unto Christ; and that beyond physical death lies our truer life within God's purpose for us.

When we let God become our ally instead of our supposed enemy, we can also become cities of peace because we overcome the cleft between our actual self and the self we long to be. We can become new creatures in Christ. We are no longer plagued by self-righteousness. We no longer try to keep the whole law in our own strength. We get what Paul Tillich calls a "transmoral conscience." This kind of conscience is not the neglect of the law, not the repressing of guilt, but the living above the law as the source of our satisfaction. The law has been fulfilled for us by God's love who now fulfills it through us. Even when our conscience condemns us, Christ is greater than our conscience.

We live, therefore, in a new freedom. This very removal of self-righteousness and anxiety releases new creative satisfactions and energies. However much we may keep sinning or failing, we come to know ever more surely that there is the promise and the power for a new level of living. As we trust God, his reality becomes real whether through sudden power or through a process of steady growth in grace. As the power of God becomes more and more our source of peace, the city of confusion gives way to the city of order; the city of strife becomes the city of peace.

Nor is such overcoming wholly personal; it is also social. The Christian not only endures his environment. He conquers it. We have lacked nerve because we have lacked Christ. God's love never fails. We fail to believe him and to accept his love. With God all things are possible, but we are not with God. A sword of man, cannot God yet turn you into a plowshare? Are the spiritual legions, ready to be summoned by prayer, less powerful than the fear that hides under military might? Cannot God gather the nations in peace and govern them with the rod of reason? When the fullness of time for world government has come, cannot his hand cause it to be? Yes, and again yes, but only according to our faith shall it be done unto us.

Is he who makes some of his children black and some white not strong enough in love to cause them to become blood brothers in Christ? Has the blood of his love been shed in vain? Can he not tear down the walls of segregation both on the books and in men's hearts? Can he who has given us both life and all we own not cause us similarly to use property for the common good through the creation of some system and social incentives beyond present choices?

Is Christ too dead to heal his own broken body? Shall his prayer that we be one go forever unheeded? Can he not give unity with freedom? Can he not give seriousness of faith with largeness of solution? Why call we Christ Lord and do not what he says? Is it not because our hearts fail us for fear? Are we not fainthearted and more disloyal in our lack of expecting than in any of our doings?

Can *any* human problem or evil be compared to the incomparable One? We are told to possess the land not by strength nor by might but by the Spirit. True humility does not consist in showing that we must not expect too much of man. Such also is worldly wisdom. True humility, beyond what man has been and now is, is to proclaim the power of God and believingly to become used by it to transform the world according to the rules of his reign.

When my son became grown and was about to leave home, I gave him a Bible as the symbol of his new maturity and responsibility. He asked me to write in it. Nothing seemed right to say. I waited until almost the very last opportunity. Then I knew what I wanted to say as his lifelong verse from his father: "And God is able to make all grace abound toward you; that ye, always having all sufficiency in all things, may abound in every good work" (II Cor. 9:8).

The Christian faith, far from allowing cities of confusion,

abounds with grace and peace. One of my favorite quotations over the years has been one of Principal A. G. Hogg's in *Redemption from the World:* "Only the assurance that the measure of the practical is never past experience, but is always God's call, can redeem us from the anxieties of the worldly-wise to a fearless life of fellowship with Christ in ever-fresh adventures of faith."

Are you, my dear friend, right now a city of confusion or are you a city filled with God's deep and abiding peace? If you have not yet found out how good God is and how much he can do for you, this is your chance. Give him your heart and trust him now for your past and for your future. The only condition for his filling you with peace is that you will decide honestly and wholeheartedly to live his life of love with and for the world. The God of love longs to give order to your life, to give you peace within. Say "yes" to him right now and you will find him ever faithful to fulfill his promises, both for you, and through you, for the world; for as Paul tells us, God is not a God of confusion but of peace.

CHAPTER 15

Victorious Although Unsuccessful

The Palm Sunday Story: LUKE 19:28-40

Recently, after preaching a sermon, I was met at the door by a man who introduced himself as a carpenter, and who asked me to explain for him the problem of evil. I began to do so, but he stopped me and said, "Oh, Dr. Ferré, I don't want to know about the problem of evil. I want to get rid of it." And then he added something I have not forgotten: "Dr. Ferré, won't you help us put the leaves back on the Tree of Life?" That startled me. In the first place, we don't take leaves and put them back on a living tree. And secondly, according to the biblical account, the trouble is not with the Tree of Life; the trouble is with us who have become separated from the Tree of Life. But I knew what he meant. We have been living for a long time in a negative age, characterized, as Tillich says, by meaninglessness, guilt, and death, and what the man wanted really was somehow to be able to turn the corner, to start again a constructive way of living.

Now I see some signs of a fresh start, some straws in the wind. At a college where I was speaking recently, the young people had put up as the motto for the week, "The Decline and Fall of Apathy." When I saw Eugene O'Neill's play *The Touch of the Poet,* I said, "The critics will murder it ruthlessly, because it is based upon love and the victory of love." But no. Much to my surprise, they gave the play positive reviews. And so it has been. For instance, at a recent gathering of the National Council on Religion and Higher Education, some of the sophisticated young college teachers said, as I have never heard them say before, "What are the redemptive aspects? Where do we go from here? How can we have something else?"

According to the biblical account of the Triumphal Entry, there are at least three ways in which we can base our lives, in which we can base history. One is, we can believe that our problems are going to be solved. Somehow or other, they are going to be solved. If only we get better science, if only we get better education, if only we get better legislation, if only, at least, we get better religion, somehow or other we can solve our problems. Or, "When I get through school," "When I get married," "When my children get through college," or, "When I retire." All the time I hear people who think that life's problems can be solved. But all life's problems can never be solved, because God has put us into this world in order to solve our problems and to learn by the solution or the meeting of these problems. We'll always have our problems.

When we learn to know that, what happens? Precisely this: we become pessimistic. We say the struggle naught avails. We perhaps turn toward Buddhism, and if not to Buddhism explicitly at least to this attitude of life, that we must do what men may, and bear what men must. The popular Broadway play *Majority of One* ends with a reference to Buddhism as the perfect serenity of the enlightened spirit.

Today we are looking for invulnerability, but that's not the way, either. The only way is to learn the secret of how to be victorious although unsuccessful. The only way is to have our Palm Sundays with the Christ, and set our face to go to Jerusalem. This is the only way we can ever solve our problems. Jesus said, "According to your faith be it done to you" (Matt. 9:29). The people of Israel wanted superficial things and God granted them their request, and sent leanness into their souls. The Pharisees wanted external recognition, and they had their reward. But to all those who were faithful it was done according to their faith.

But you say, "Was it? Was it? What about Jesus? Was it according to his faith that Jesus, if we may speak humanly, was crucified on the town dump for what he did? Did

Socrates, who cared for nothing but the people and the respect for law, get anything but the hemlock? What happened to St. Francis, writing his hymn of joy, with rats running over his legs in the middle of the courtyard? What happened to Rembrandt, forsaken, unrecognized? What happened to Bach, some of his music picked out of the ashcan by a maid?

"Have the people who have given to the world received what they should? Can we honestly stand here and claim that it was done unto them according to their faith?"

I am going to answer, "Yes." Because what Jesus sought was to do his Father's will. It was not external recognition. What Jesus sought to do was to find the victory that went beyond any human success, because it was lodged in the very heart of God and in the very deepest meaning of history. And this is exactly what happened to Jesus, and he had, in spite of all suffering—and all who try it will have it—in spite of all suffering, that inner triumph of being victorious although unsuccessful.

I have one great abiding conviction: that more than anything today the world needs the people who know the secret of accepting the will of God, no matter what happens to them, who have the faith that they can receive grace to help in time of need. Those who are able to identify themselves with God's will for humanity and to go beyond their own personal little selves and what people think of them, to go beyond their own family, their own group, their own denomination, their own nature, and to come out completely and without hesitation for the universal will of God, as he has shown his love in the faith and the suffering of Jesus Christ—those people not only dare to take up the cross, but in doing so receive the grace to be expendable.

My wife thinks grace before meals ought to include mention of the food and perhaps the hands that prepared it. She says that that is what grace is for. But one day when I invited a distinguished guest to ask the blessing, he bowed his head and said only, "O God, give us grace to be expendable." I have never forgotten that prayer, and I have prayed and prayed for that grace.

But what else? Is that all that is needed to gain a victory? No. If it were not for these people, these countless numbers, and you among them, I hope, who long for the grace to be expendable, and who are victorious although unsuccessful, the world would not even be what it is now. They become the leaven of the world, a leaven that a woman took and hid in three mesaures of meal until all was leavened. The world depends continuously upon the people who are its leaven because they have made the will of God basic to their lives.

The victory of Jesus in the Palm Sunday story was, in one sense, a true victory not only because of the resurrection. I believe in the reality of the resurrection. I believe that the events connected with the resurrection and the overcoming by God of sin, law, and death are history's greatest triumph and eternity's greatest revelation. I believe in the resurrection.

But I believe in something besides resurrection. I believe that it is not only possible but certain that lives go on according to the faith in terms of the leaven which is given to history. But often we do not see the result. And therefore we often become discouraged.

May I share two incidents in my life when something happened that might never have come to my attention? Once I was asked to preach at Chapel Hill, University of North Carolina, opening a series of Sunday evening services. Since it was the beginning of university services there, the people in charge were anxious that there be a good fellowship, a good turnout, and an important service.

That night Cordell Hull visited the campus and the president entertained him with an "open house" for all, with refreshments, and it did cut into our crowd. Nevertheless, although crushed in my human expectations, I went home feeling a deep victory in spite of the small turnout, believing in my heart that God had shown mighty power even though I could not see any results.

Several years later there came a letter from Switzerland, from one of the outstanding young men in the World Council of Churches, saying that he had been there that night, and that it was the great commitment point in his life. He said, "You'll never know what happened to me that night." This letter might never have been written. We seldom learn these things.

On another occasion I was praying for a Southern Baptist minister, a dedicated Christian who was being criticized for his theological and social views to the point of persecution. I had never met him but I had heard about him. I wrote him a postcard and mailed it. Much later, when I was teaching in Oxford and had long ago forgotten the card, the doorbell rang and this man stood there. He said, "Dr. Ferré, I want to thank you." Then he added, "I had gotten to the point where I thought I was going to have a nervous breakdown, and my wife and I agreed that I could not continue in the ministry. We were sitting discouraged in the living room, and I went to the mailbox, and there was the card! God wiped the windshield clean! God wiped the windshield clean! And I started over again."

Oh, the things that we never know! We may feel that we are unsuccessful, but if we genuinely trust him we shall be victorious far beyond known results. God's word never comes back void, the Bible teaches.

Finally, Christ will be victorious. He who rode into Jerusalem to die is going to ride the final triumphant march, for as the Book of Revelation says, the beasts all came up on the shore against the Lamb (that represents the love of God), came up to devour that little Lamb, but the Lamb overcame them, and all that were with him, called, and chosen, and faithful.

So I believe that God will win, and we shall win with him if we trust him. "For the things which are seen are temporal; but the things which are not seen are eternal" (II Cor. 4:18). "Whatsoever is born of God overcometh the world" (I John 5:4), for "the world passeth away, and the lust thereof, but he that doeth the will of God abideth forever" (I John 2:17). In the meantime we can be victorious, although unsuccessful. To the victorious Christ and to God be all the glory, majesty, and honor, now and forevermore. Amen.

CHAPTER 16
Toward Spiritual Renewal

No other foundation can anyone lay than that which is laid, which is Jesus Christ. Let each man take care how he builds upon it. I CORINTHIANS 3:11, 10

No one can responsibly deny the crucial nature of our times. There are several systems of atomic annihilation already at hand. We are manufacturing pilotless planes to carry destruction by means of germ or chemical warfare. The small nations may soon possess atomic weapons with a high probability of their early use. In the meantime we suffer internal paralysis of will to cope effectively with our situation while all the time moral rot is eating away the foundations of our civilization.

We need the church to lead us toward spiritual renewal, but first the church must itself experience a new Pentecost. As early as Paul's time, as shown by First Corinthians 16, Pentecost was a day on the church calendar. Today we need to put it once more at a foremost place not only in our church calendar but in our total lives. Pentecost transforms all of life. Emphasis on the Spirit in salvation and sanctification apart from man's total life in society and nature becomes false pietism. We can use our heritage to make holy history for today if we take with full seriousness God's invitation to spiritual renewal.

I

Our text affirms that the foundation for such renewal is laid once for all in Jesus Christ, but that each person must continually take care how he builds on it. Spiritual renewal can come only as individual members of the church become renewed.

In our home where my wife is a Yankee and I am Swedish born there is a saying, "Don't be a Swede!" My wife, generalizing, I am sure, on too small a basis for judgment, has the idea that Swedes take things personally. Be that as it may, I want each of you to take your religion personally. You can join me in the blessed privilege, not of being Swedish, but of taking your Christian faith personally.

Augustine spoke of God as caring for all as though they were each one and as caring for each one as though he were all. Whitehead defined religion as what each individual does with his own solitariness. The Negro spiritual we all know: "It's me, it's me, O Lord, standing in the need of prayer." There is no divided responsibility in faith. Each person must take care how he builds on the one and only foundation; for spiritual renewal comes through him.

Will you, then, take trust personally? Will you stop trying to become good and let God remake you? Will you give the Holy Spirit a chance? Moralism kills the church. It quenches the Spirit. The early Methodists, for instance, feared "salvation by works" like the plague. To depend on works is to court self-righteousness and to block spiritual renewal.

Christ is the only foundation. We build in trust because of the grace of God. If the church is to experience renewal it must regain the vision and experience of God's grace. We used to sing:

> Amazing grace! how sweet the sound
>   That saved a wretch like me!
> I once was lost, but now am found,
>   Was blind, but now I see.
>
> 'Twas grace that taught my heart to fear,
>   And grace my fears relieved;

How precious did that grace appear
The hour I first believed!

Whatever shortcomings John Newton's life had, in this hymn
he has struck the bedrock of Christian experience: the grace
of God in Christ.

When you take trust personally God changes your life by
his grace, but more than that, you become a channel for
spiritual renewal. This world is like a human body where
all the cells are interrelated. Push the hypodermic needle in
the arm and the bloodstream carries the toxin-antitoxin to
heal the diphtheria throat. The whole world is related
through God's presence in creation in such a way that every
part is related to all the rest.

I should like to repeat Teilhard de Chardin's word of
hope on this point, namely, that "immensity represents the
action common to all atoms. The volume of each of them is
the volume of the universe. The atom is no longer the microscopic, closed world we have imagined to ourselves. It is the
infinitesimal center of the world itself."

So it is. The problem of affecting the world, therefore, is
not a matter of time and space so much as the quality of the
life we live.

What matters most is the kind of faith we have. When we
open up heedlessly in full trust to the grace of God for
spiritual renewal, there is no limit to what God can do
through us to change the world. "God is able to make all
grace to abound" not only to us but just as much through
us for spiritual renewal.

Will you also take prayer personally? Stop saying prayers
and begin to pray. Saying prayers is secondhand praying.
When you pray your whole being relies on God and within
that relationship the Holy Spirit prompts your prayer.
Prayer is the full acceptance of God's will. It is losing one's
life to find it in God. It is creative passivity. It is finding the
power to belong to true community and to live in line with
our destiny.

Prayer is at the same time our identification with the whole world. It is our unreserved involvement in the world's problems and pains, its hopes and attainments for its inclusive and concrete good. Prayer is our participation in the world's life at its center where decisions are made and where the results must be met. The praying person becomes a link between God and man, God's channel through our freedom where his grace can flow into the world's fulfillment.

Prayer is basically our resting in God. God's rest stimulates the world's work. God's silence speaks potently in the midst of the world's shouting. God's quiet Spirit writes the most constraining letters. We have tried too long to live without prayer, to work without prayer, to rest without prayer. Prayer is the power of God's presence for the world in the midst of its turmoils, dissolving false tensions and creating constructive endeavor. Try prayer through trust. God will not fail you.

Will you also take witnessing personally? Try to witness by your own struggle and meet your own defeat. Try to witness by trusting and what you become will thunder God's presence. Christ claimed to be the truth. He linked truth with a way and a life. Try walking in the way of trust and living within the reality of prayer and you will find that God's presence in you cannot be hid. Your heart will be full of God's presence and you cannot help both doing and speaking the truth.

Bishop James A. Pike has written a book, *Doing the Truth*. Truth is doing. But it is a matter of doing only if it is prompted by God's being in us. When God is in us our actions conform to Christian standards. Christian life is a matter of character but of character moved by concern. Christian "doing the truth" is conduct motivated by compassion. Doing Christ's truth is character in the service of community. Unless we live according to Christian principles we shall neither be nor do the truth, but Christian principles are love's directives in unlimited openness to the joys and sorrows of others.

When witnessing is first by being and then by doing, our saying also becomes genuine. Then our words stop being empty and false. Then our whole selves speak and our neighbors are truly addressed. The world has stopped listening because most speech is self-protective and self-promoting. The world's words center in the self no matter how much that self may then pretend interest in others.

When we speak in the words given by the Holy Spirit we speak in the demonstration of the authenticity that results from a full union of being, doing, and speaking the truth. Will you stop letting the preacher be the only constant witness—and that all too often from a safe pulpit and hid behind clerical garb? Will you in the ordinary ways of life find a way of letting God witness through you, even through your failures, even through your stuttering and stammering his truth?

Spiritual renewal can come only when an aroused laity will become God's constant medium for witnessing to the reality and relevance of the Gospel. The Gospel alone fully fits the world's needs.

II

Spiritual renewal must also come through the Christian family. Let each family see how it builds on the only foundation for spiritual renewal, even Jesus Christ, the Son of God's love. The family obviously cannot take the place of any person. In God's wisdom no person or group can take the place of anyone else. Salvation is both corporate and personal. But the family occupies a place of peculiar importance in God's dispensation, standing as it does between the individual person and the inclusive fellowship of the church. The family is God's intensive mode of community where the ultimate and the intimate meet.

The family is the world in miniature. In the family come together man's main concerns. The spiritual and the social, the economic and the political structures and functions of the family resemble, on a small scale, the problems of the world. The family is the testing ground for life in the large. Whoever can solve his problems genuinely within the family will seldom fail in the world. Whatever family can exhibit its overcoming of the world within itself can the most fully help that world.

Peculiarly enough, the family is a constant unity of human community. Its forms may vary but its intimate nature and function in human society remain the same. Man's general community in human history has changed from early tribal relations to modern man's consciousness of world responsibility. Wider and wider has grown the human community in history. But the family base has secured man's permanence of relationships. God has a special purpose for the family.

We are all born in a family and reared in a family. Our affections are colored for life within our family living. To change the world we must change the family. Without change at the center of life's beginning and growth there will be no effective change anywhere else. Our mothers are the most strategic people for letting God's new age come. Don't ever say, "I'm only a housewife." No, homemaker. No, much more, you are the mother of humanity.

For God to become real and for spiritual renewal to go deep we need parents who care enough for their children to put first things first. To live for God and the world in the family by living for each member of the family, and for the family as a community, is life's central task. The inner circle of human community is constantly the family. Change the family and we change the world. Win the family for Christ and the world will find him, too.

The family judges us most searchingly, but it is also the place where we can become the most effective. It is impossible to fool the family. You may be a hero to multitudes and looked down on by your own family. They may know you are sham. Or you may be a monster to countless people through false propaganda, while your own family who knows you loves and admires you. Will you become genuine in your spiritual renewal in the face of your family?

I remember attending the funeral of one of America's spiritual leaders. In the family car following the hearse an important guest was tactless enough to ask a teen-age daughter of the deceased whether her father at home was really such a saint as he was hailed. Without hesitation, in a painful hour of her life, she replied tenderly, "He was no more than average." Our children know us more deeply than our reputation, be it good or bad!

Over and over again I keep repeating to myself the saying reported to me of a sociologist to the effect that two or three genuinely committed people could change a church. Jesus said that where two or three are gathered in his name he himself will be in their midst. What cannot a family do if it becomes possessed through and through by the Holy Spirit! We cannot control the world. Can the family be persuaded to make completely central to its life this task of spiritual renewal? Will you take the spiritual dare and try changing your church by making it your priority as a family through trust, prayer, and witness?

God's judgment and God's grace can combine in your family to produce an inaugurated eschatology. By this I mean a fragment of the fulfilled future. God came in Christ to create a new community to the end of the world and to the end of time. He can do an unbelievable job in your family if you let him.

I feel myself both more judged and more rewarded by God's grace in the family than anywhere else. I am not worthy of the kind of family I have received. But one thing I know. If I had lived God's love more trustingly and more genuinely there is no limit to what God could have done in such a family as mine. More and more I acknowledge God's reality and increasingly at the same time I confess my own failure. Will you join me in making the priority of family life the spiritual renewal of the church?

Our concern is with spiritual renewal. The family must

take its full part in this concern. It can do so only within the grace of God. Only the family trusting the grace of God can play its part in the renewal of the church. It must be a worshiping family. Family worship for me is high celebration. In the family in which I was brought up the worship of God was central. My parents perhaps had many failings, but they never failed us in the seriousness with which they took family worship.

In our own experience as a family we have lived around the family altar. How good it is to start the day together singing great Christian hymns, reading the Bible together, and praying aloud, one and all, for God's will in the world and for the meeting of our own needs in God's way.

Will you join us in building a family altar, and, if you have one, in putting more fuel on the fire? Begin where you are. Make a church in your own house. That is biblical. If you cannot all pray aloud, why not begin with using *The Upper Room* or some other daily devotional guide. Read and sing and pray as you can and as you grow.

If you make such family worship life's primary appointment you will find life in the family transformed by it. Of course, the children like to sleep on Saturday mornings or when they are home from school or college on vacation. If the prayers are real, however, they will rejoice in a family that thinks enough of its worship to get them up for it. Don't be inflexible, of course; prove sometimes that you are not legalistic about it. Don't let devotions degenerate to a duty. How you carry on such worship depends on you, but you can't help the family more than by making its worship central.

Worship together depends on the strength of your personal prayer life. You cannot rest your personal prayer life on that of the family. Will you learn to pray faithfully for the other members of the family? In prayer you enter imaginatively into their lives; you pray for grace to let them live their own lives in fellowship, you grope for ways of helping them without intruding in their lives.

What a difference such praying for the other members of the family makes! How significantly you enter into their lives. How willingly you let them alone to grow and learn when that is best for them. How the problems and projects of each becomes a family concern.

No one lives lonely any more. How easily all members of the family can share their joys in a circle of primary support and not of primary competition. The deepest drives of life can find discipline and direction within family living if each member is continually supported by common prayers and individual prayers in humble acceptance and concern for each and all.

The family can be an unparalleled gift from God. If the world passes you by or hurts you in your deepest longings, you are still buoyed up and steadied by family love. The Christian family lives for God's will in the whole world as it enters into God's love for his whole family of man. The local Christian family becomes part of the church family without boundaries, and having turned toward God, it turns back by his grace to face with arms wide open the needs of the neighborhood and of the world. Family prayers range from God to all the world and down to the smallest immediate need.

What matters the most is where your treasure is. If your treasure is steadily God's longing for spiritual attainment for his whole world, your family life becomes lifted and led to that end. If you are to take your task of spiritual renewal with full seriousness, you must make decisive the spiritual renewal of your own family.

Will you let God renew his church and help to turn world history through your family? Don't keep the Father waiting. Bless him now by your firm and lasting decision.

III

But personal and family renewal are not enough. We are speaking of spiritual renewal in Christian terms. This means the renewal of God's people, of the church, of Christ's body. Spiritual renewal involves letting Christ be Lord. He must become the effective head of the church. Our aim is to renew the church of God and through it to offer the world a new chance for civilization.

When God renews his people he makes them see what the true nature of the church is. The church is founded on Christ. Our text is plain: there is no other foundation on which to build. The only foundation is Christ and Christ is nothing less than God's presence on earth in human form. Christ is God incarnate. Christ is the Word made flesh.

The church is likewise God's presence on earth in the Christian community. The church is not primarily sociological but theological. It is not only God's work but his presence; it is not only his representative but his own dwelling among men. To be sure, the church does not have the same power over sin that Jesus did. How utterly far the church falls short of the glory of God! Christ was in Jesus pre-eminently and organically. But unless God is the head of the church there is no church, for Christ alone can be the head of the church, and Christ is God's presence on earth.

Jesus Christ by being God's holy love on earth founded the church. Jesus Christ by teaching God's unlimited, outgoing love founded the church. Jesus Christ by establishing a community within his love and through the power of the resurrection founded the church.

He gathered a human community, a group of followers, a band of wandering disciples, but nothing could withstand the community where all had the same care for one another and where the whole community preached the Gospel to the ends of the world. Jesus Christ is the head of the church because God's presence found power in him for the open, inclusive, concerned community. The Christian church is the community of God's ever-faithful love living for the whole world and to the end of earthly time.

The head of the church is Christ. In the body God works through the Holy Spirit. Christ is the unity of God's love

above and for the church. The Holy Spirit is the diversity
of God's love in the unity of the common body. Thus God
comes into the church both through Christ the head and
through the Holy Spirit, his corporate presence. The church
was founded on Pentecost by the presence and power of the
Holy Spirit. The disciples waited in Jerusalem for the return
of their Lord. He came as head of the church to his body,
the church, by the reality and work of the Holy Spirit.

The Holy Spirit guided the original church and made it
grow. God gave the increase. Therefore the early church
celebrated Pentecost. Neither Christmas nor Easter is mentioned as such in the New Testament. They came to be celebrated a good deal later, but already in First Corinthians 16,
as we saw, Pentecost is mentioned as a date on the calendar.
Please ponder this fact. Relive it.

We shall have no renewal of the church till we declare
Christ to be Lord, but we can do so only in the power of
the Holy Spirit. What is lacking today is the reality and
power of the Holy Spirit. We shall not have spiritual renewal
until we, too, wait in prayer for our Lord. When he comes
he will come with Pentecost, with his glorious power in the
church testifying to the head of the church, the living
Christ.

All talk about Christ is the mumbling of clichés until the
Holy Spirit possess us and use us. Let us wait in trust for the
Holy Spirit to create us a community of grace. Let us wait
in trust for the Holy Spirit to empower us in life and teaching. Let the Word and Sacrament be no longer rites to dull
the Spirit but celebrations of the living Christ within the
presence and power of the Holy Spirit.

I have a concrete suggestion to this end. We must restore
core-Christianity, through intimate life and worship in small
groups. A peculiarly powerful historical case in hand is the
original Methodist Class Meeting. The power of yesterday's
church was the prayer meeting. It was the thermometer of the
life of the church. But many modern changes in life have
killed the prayer meeting. To some extent the death of the

prayer meeting signifies the death of vital personal faith sufficiently general to sustain such an act of regular worship.
From another angle our knowledge of psychology and our
changed sociological conditions have caused the demise of the
prayer meeting. Most of us believe it can hardly be revived
for our churches in its original form.

Nevertheless we need the more intimate form and power
of the faith. How can we get it? Some try study groups, some
discussion groups, some social gatherings, some prayer part-
ners. The Methodist Class Meeting combined the need for
small groups in worship, in prayer, in study, in discipline,
and in confession. For a few glorious months I participated in
such a group in England among Methodists with a Primitive
Methodist background. In it I knew the warmth of intimate
fellowship, the openness of confession, the seriousness of
worship, and the diligence of study. I believe that the class
meeting can be re-created to meet our modern conditions and
that through it God can create both depth and intensity of
spiritual renewal.

The church cannot be the church, however, without ex-
periencing concern for the world. It is called to preach the
Gospel to the world, to evangelize it. It is also called to teach
the world the truth of Christ, to educate it. With equal insistence it is also called to be socially responsible.

The church is in, but not of, the world. Therefore it has
light and leaven to offer the world. The church is not the
world, but lives by the grace of God a new creation. As such
it offers salt to the world. The church is called to preserve
what is good, to illumine what is evil, and to change the
world by the interpenetration of its healing presence.

Such responsibility for the world in all its social, economic,
and political problems is not the heart of the Gospel but it
belongs to the very heartbeat of the Gospel. The heart of the
Gospel is God's ever-faithful and inclusive love in Christ, but
such love has no meaning unless it expresses itself to those
in need everywhere and of every kind.

In our world today the church that has nothing to offer a

world in peril of immediate destruction has no Gospel. The
church that does not care about God's creatures and creation
itself is not Christian. The church without a Gospel for society is simply sham.

We must destroy war or war will destroy us. A new inclusive kind of community came in Christ. It is our only
alternative to deterioration and destruction. Let the inclusive
human society become inclusively concerned, using only such
police power as is necessary within its inclusive community.
We have war with us yet because the Church has failed its
mission. It has falsely detached souls from society. It has
isolated spirit from body.

We must work now for an inclusively effective world
organization of power. We need world law and world rule.
Militarism must die.

It may not do so until we kill the spirit of capitalism. We
need to destroy greed and corruption in politics. A start to
that end is the use of property more inclusively both within
our nation and to the ends of the world. What that will
involve politically I do not know and care only secondarily.
If we have the need of all the people and of the whole world
on our Christian hearts, God will guide us into the proper
working out of the problems of order.

We do not want atheistic Marxism. It is becoming a giant
of power and of unimagined growth. What have we to offer?
Atom bombs will not keep back an aroused humanity. Let
us answer with creative concern to do away with oppressive
militarism and exploitive property relations, and release the
world's goods for the world's people in faith and freedom. We
must kill war, the killer of mankind.

We must destroy racialism as well. We have made a beginning. A Methodist minister walks with a Catholic priest in
New Orleans to proclaim the Gospel of brotherhood, risking
his own little daughter to the hostile mobs that jeer at racial
co-operation. The Gospel is big enough for the full job. I
know no other power big enough for the task than God's love
for the common good. Let the church itself wake up to the

lateness of the hour. We face increased racial destructiveness or the dawn of racial acceptance.

In the neighborhood in which I live, a typical, comfortable upper middle-class neighborhood, four Negro families have recently moved in. I feel that our neighborhood is now more sacred because it is truly more human. Although the neighborhood is predominantly Christian, our two immediate neighbors are Jewish. Some apologize for the fact that the neighborhood "isn't what it used to be." A few racial "causists," of course, glory in it. We simply accept such cultural mixing as genuinely human, rejoicing only in the fact that we live together not only in peace but in friendship. No spiritual renewal can come until we are cleansed of prejudice and live normally the reality of the Gospel of God's love for all.

If we are to find spiritual renewal our whole lives as people must be involved. Too long have we lived according to secular values. We have felt and acted like the world. Spiritual renewal involves a dimension of genuineness in all human relations. We must dare to become fully and worthily human. The church is God's inclusive community of creative and co-operative concern.

The church is no moralistic in-group. It is no defensively group-centered organization. It does not live by comparing itself with other groups. It lives in the open grace of God for fullness of community and knows a human fulfillment that is real in personal, family, and community relationships.

We must get rid of conformity to the secular world. We must become transformed by the renewing of our minds within the perfect will of God for the world. Let there be less of the world in the church and there will be more of the church in the world.

As we dedicate ourselves to spiritual renewal, many voices will warn us not to go the whole way in our commitment. In Second Chronicles 18 there is the story of the false prophets versus the true. The false prophets were all conformists and conformers. They advised the king to do what was in his heart and God would be with him. The true prophet stood alone demanding a drastic change of ways. The king followed the false. The false prophets were possessed with lying spirits to lead him astray. The true asked God for repentance and spiritual renewal.

Today, similarly, I can offer no hope for a safe future. All I can say is that if we repent and reform, God can use us beyond all thought for the salvation of the world. God is able to save.

In First Samuel 14 Jonathan is reported to face a hopeless situation, but he turned the tide because of his conviction that "nothing can hinder the Lord from saving by many or by few."

Do you remember how Aaron, in Numbers 16, when the plague was spreading in the camp, had to stand between the living and the dead until the plague stopped? Today we are in the same situation. We must withstand the plague of destruction by the power of spiritual renewal, trusting that God can save even by the few.

Once David numbered all the people for war, but he was not allowed to number the Levites, the servants of God. The reason for that, said the late Methodist Bishop William Alfred Quayle, was that God was not counting them but counting on them. God does not count you, but counts on you.

The church and the family need spiritual renewal. Until they are renewed the world cannot be changed toward the creative and co-operative community that will usher in God's new age. But you are the key to the family and the church. I put the offer of God's presence and power right up to you. You can be used beyond your every imagination to renew the spirit of the church. Will you decide to put your whole life in God's hands to be used by him and will you persevere and grow in the power of the Holy Spirit? Right now we are fast heading for destruction. But with God's help we can turn about and face a new day.

Spiritual renewal is up to you. Christ help you!

22139